© 2016

Substitute Teaching Division, STEDI.org

ISBN: 978-0-9821657-3-7 • Substitute Teacher Handbook • 9th Edition

These materials are for use by substitute teachers. Copies of handout pages are for classroom use by the owner of this handbook and does not include training workshops. Contact STEDI.org for additional handbooks at STEDI.org, PO Box 3470, Logan, UT 84321-3470, info@STEDI.org, or at **www.STEDI.org.**

Written permission is required by the Substitute Teaching Division of STEDI.org to reproduce any of these materials in any form.

PREFACE:
WHAT THIS HANDBOOK IS ALL ABOUT

*S*ubstitute teaching is a crucial component of quality education in the school system. It is a rare teacher who never needs a substitute for either personal or professional reasons, and so principals, teachers, parents, and students all come to highly value an excellent substitute teacher. Research has shown that, on average, a student spends over one full year with a substitute teacher by the time the student graduates from high school. As a skilled substitute teacher, you can make a significant positive impact on the schools and students you work with.

Regardless of whether or not you are a certified teacher, you can still become an expert in substitute teaching. Successful teachers are those who have either consciously, or subconsciously, mastered necessary skills and classroom techniques. By learning and practicing the skills in this handbook, you can become the kind of substitute teacher who can schedule your assignments weeks in advance, have students ask when you're coming back to their class, and even have teachers and parents request that you're hired full time!

In order to make the content concise and practical, most of the theory behind the skills and strategies here has been intentionally left out. However, you can feel confident that the suggestions to come in the following chapters have been thoroughly researched, documented, and field-tested over the past four decades in order to give you the finest training that educational research has to offer.

Research conducted by the Substitute Teaching Institute at Utah State University has found the following:

- The number one request by substitute teachers is that they are trained in skills to successfully manage inappropriate behavior situations.
- The number one trait of a successful substitute teacher is the use of a *SubPack* or resource kit.
- The number one request by permanent teachers and school personnel is that substitute teachers be prepared and professional.
- The number one request by students is that substitute teachers present stimulating lessons and exciting fill-in activities.

Remember:

The information in this handbook is not intended to replace the rules and regulations of the district. Use only those suggestions and activities from this handbook that do not conflict with the district's policies and established practices.

Contributing Authors

GEOFFREY G. SMITH:

Mr. Smith is the director of the Substitute Teaching Division of STEDI.org and was the founding director of the Substitute Teaching Institute at Utah State University (STI/ USU). He has been the principal investigator for STEP-IN (Substitute Teacher Educational Program Initiative) and has also led several other research projects relating to substitute teaching. He is the publisher of the *Substitute Teacher Handbook* (U.S.A.), *Supply Teacher Handbook* (U.K.), *SubJournal* and the *SubExchange* newsletter. He holds an MBA in Public Administration, a Master of Educational Economics, and has been involved with substitute teacher professional development and research since 1990.

GLENN LATHAM:

Dr. Latham was a professor emeritus of special education at Utah State University (USU) and served as a principal investigator at the Mountain Plains Regional Resource Center. His internationally acclaimed work is founded on a system of principles, strategies, and skills developed, tested, and proven in his 35 years of continuous research and trial. Dr. Latham defined this behavior model in over 250 technical research papers, reports, journal articles, presentations, books, and chapters in books relating to behavior management at home and in schools.

MAX L. LONGHURST:

Dr. Longhurst was the elementary education specialist at Utah State University. He writes, field-tests, and develops materials for substitute teachers and conducts seminars and training sessions for school personnel and educators. Having been in the classroom both as a permanent teacher and a substitute teacher, his experience provides practical applications for teaching and learning strategies.

JESSICA L. SMITH:

Substitute Teacher Trainer at the Substitute Teaching Division of STEDI.org, Jessica has also worked both as a permanent teacher and a substitute teacher. She trains thousands of substitute teachers nationwide through webinars, online, and onsite training. Jessica maintains the Bus Stop Blog and the SubSuggestions Newsletter available at STEDI.org.

A SPECIAL THANKS TO:

Barbara Haines, Robert L. Morgan, Linda Robinson, Carla Kaplan, Danielle Macfarlane, Michelle Johnson, Diane Iverson, Cynthia Murdock, Janine Alvarado, Luz María Westphal, Peter Brooks, and Tanya Bagley.

Table of Contents

CHAPTER THREE:

THE PROFESSIONAL SUBSTITUTE TEACHER

CHAPTER FOUR:

SPECIAL EDUCATION

CHAPTER FIVE:

OTHER THINGS YOU SHOULD KNOW

CHAPTER SIX:

FILL-IN ACTIVITIES

Why become an approved

✔ GAIN SELF-CONFIDENCE
You will gain the self-assurance to teach any class or age group.

Preparation is power. As an approved STEDI-Ready Substitute, you will master the skills to enter any classroom with confidence. At STEDI, we did a national survey and discovered that the #1 request by substitute teachers is training in how to successfully manage inappropriate behavior. We will teach you to be an approved STEDI-Ready sub by focusing on these basic skills:

- Classroom Management
- Teaching Strategies
- The Professional Substitute
- Special Education
- Fill-in Activities

(Oh, and you will learn to avoid those nasty traps that substitute teachers fall into!)

✔ LEARN FUNDAMENTAL SKILLS
You will acquire all the skills you need to be an exceptional substitute.

An approved STEDI-Ready Substitute teacher knows how to:
• Recognize appropriate behavior
• Ignore inappropriate behavior
• Set and teach clear expectations
• Handle consequential student behavior
• Effectively get and keep students on task
• Present lesson material in an engaging way
• Fill in time when the lesson plans end early
• Maintain a risk-free environment
• Inspire and motivate students to excel
• Create a useful "SubPack" resource kit

Plus, you will also join a network of professional substitutes where you can share lesson plans and activity ideas! We all win.

✔ BECOME A TRUE PROFESSIONAL
You will be head and shoulders above other substitutes.

Even if your district does not cover the tuition for you to become a STEDI-Ready Substitute, the benefits will pay off in the short- and long-run. There is a difference between a "normal" substitute and an approved STEDI-Ready Substitute. Investing in your own training shows that you believe in your professional development. You will be a better teacher. You will be a top performer. You will demonstrate your desire to enter any classroom truly prepared. A STEDI-Ready Substitute is the mark of a true professional.

✔ IMPRESS YOUR EMPLOYER
You will show school districts you are serious about teaching.

Administrators are extremely impressed with substitute teachers who take it upon themselves to receive training, particularly those who do so at their own expense. When you pass the SubAssessment and earn your SubDiploma, make sure to add it to your resume and let your school district know of your academic accomplishment. Many districts reward those who successfully become STEDI-Ready by increasing the frequency of job assignments and even giving pay raises.

429 South Main Street
Logan, Utah 84321
www.STEDI.org

STEDI *Ready!* substitute teacher?

✓ RECEIVE ONGOING TRAINING

You will discover fresh ideas with our biweekly updates.

Your training does not end by earning your SubDiploma. We continue to give you even more ideas with our biweekly "SubSuggestions Newsletter." Every other week, we give you tips for improving your teaching skills. These SubSuggestions focus on all facets of substitute teaching: getting the attention of your students, handling a "tough" setting, and working in special education. Plus, we share with you new fill-in activities that keep your students occupied and learning at the same time.

✓ GET OFFERED A JOB

You will get offered a job as a substitute

School districts love Stead-Ready substitutes As an approved STEDI-Ready sub, you will get a substitute teaching job. Simply complete our SubSkills Online Training Course or read the entire Substitute Teacher Handbook, earn your STEDI SubDiploma, and meet your district's hiring requirements.

Your next step?
Go to STEDI.org get ready to pass the SubAssessment and earn your SubDiploma.

100+ bonus classroom activities—FREE

Because you purchased this Substitute Teacher Handbook, you now have access to 100+ activity ideas and worksheets to use in a pinch…**FREE!**

HOW TO DOWNLOAD

Visit **STEDI.org/Handbook**.

At checkout, enter **HANDBOOK13** in the "Coupon Code" area

Thank you for letting STEDI.org help prepare you to be a great substitute teacher!

CLASSROOM MANAGEMENT

*H*aving a well-polished set of behavior management skills is essential for success in the classroom. Chapter One explains four principles of human behavior, five management skills, and several powerful strategies to help you effectively manage the learning environment. Developed by Dr. Glenn Latham, the skills presented are statistically proven to prevent 94 percent of inappropriate student behavior and provide strategies to handle the remaining six percent.

As you come to understand and apply these techniques, you will increase your ability to:
- Effectively get and keep students on task.
- Maintain a risk-free environment.
- Communicate expectations.
- Respond non-coercively to consequential student behavior.

As with any new skill, classroom management takes time and practice to master. Just as knowing the rules of the road doesn't necessarily mean you can drive a car safely... employing classroom management skills might not come naturally or be easy at first. Eventually it can become second nature and will be well worth the effort.

Dr. Glenn Latham, Professor of Education and behavior analyst

"Every learner who enters our classroom should leave a better and more able person. When the learning environment is managed properly, this is more a possibility than it is a simple ideal."

Note:

The classroom management skills and strategies outlined are also especially effective in at-risk and special needs classes.

Four Principles of Human Behavior

Principles are truths not limited by age, time, location, or situation. Once you become familiar with behavior principles, you will see them illustrated all around you—between parents and children, in stores, on playgrounds, at family events, etc. It is impossible to write a book that covers every classroom scenario you may encounter as a teacher. However, when you know and understand these principles, your actions can change, increasing the likelihood that the students in your class will behave appropriately.

PRINCIPLE ONE:
Behavior is largely a product of its immediate environment.

The classroom environment teachers create through the expectations they set will influence students more than outside factors do. This allows teachers to take control and influence the students' behavior in their classrooms. If a student is acting out, the teacher should pay special attention to altering the classroom (immediate environment). If the teacher changes the classroom, the behavior of the students will change.

Example:

Outside the Classroom: A car (student) is damaged by traveling along the same bumpy road (immediate environment) every day. No matter how much money or time is spent fixing the car, unless the road is fixed (teacher skills), the car (student) will always need repairs.

Inside the Classroom: The same students can behave perfectly for one teacher and disrespectfully towards another teacher.

PRINCIPLE TWO:
Behavior is strengthened or weakened by its consequences.

When disruptive behavior becomes a pattern, it is important to take a look at what is happening immediately after the behavior. Attention from a teacher is a powerful motivator for most students. If you pay more attention to students who are behaving appropriately than to students who are not, you will be encouraging appropriate behavior.

Example:

Outside the Classroom: At the grocery store a child doesn't get the candy he wants and throws a temper tantrum. His mom gives him the candy to make him be quiet. This reinforces the behavior by teaching him he can get what he wants by throwing a tantrum.

In the Classroom: Lizzy yells out the answer to a question and the teacher acknowledges her answer. The next time she wants to answer a question, Lizzy will most likely yell out the answer again.

However, if Lizzy yells out the answer and the teacher ignores it and calls on Cameron who is raising his hand, Lizzy will see that she needs to raise her hand in order to get the teacher's attention.

PRINCIPLE THREE:
Behavior ultimately responds better to positive than to negative consequences.

People respond better to positive encouragement than to negative processes. Think of the tasks you do every day; if someone thanks you or compliments you on how well you did, you feel much more likely to continue the task. As a teacher, you can help stop undesirable behavior and increase appropriate behavior by genuinely reinforcing the latter.

Example:

Outside the Classroom: Next time you attend a sporting event, notice how much the phenomenon of "home field advantage" can influence the team. When a team hears cheers and support from their own fans, instead of heckling and negativity, they are more likely to win the game.

In the Classroom: As a teacher was trying to line up his students, he kept asking Caden to get in line, but Caden wouldn't move. After asking two times, the teacher changed his tactic. He thanked Sophia and Mark for getting in line so quickly. Almost immediately after the positive interaction, Caden jumped in line. After 30 seconds, the teacher then thanked Caden for standing so quietly in line.

PRINCIPLE FOUR:
Whether a behavior has been punished or reinforced is known only by the course of that behavior in the future.

If an appropriate behavior is repeated, it has been reinforced. If an undesirable behavior is repeated, it too has been reinforced. If an undesirable behavior has discontinued, it has been properly disciplined.

The only way to tell if a response to a behavior is punishing or reinforcing is to watch what happens to the behavior in the future. What is considered a punishment to one person may reinforce and perpetuate a behavior in another.

Example:

Outside the Classroom: Robyn walked into the bathroom to find her husband cleaning it. She immediately gave her husband a huge hug and thanked him for making the bathroom look so great. The next Saturday the bathroom was cleaned again.

In the Classroom: Two students are talking in the back of the classroom and not working on their assignments. The teacher moves closer to the students. One student stops talking and begins working. The other student keeps talking. The teacher realizes that proximity wasn't a punishment to the second student and tries another strategy. The teacher quietly says to the student, *"What do I expect you to be doing now?"* The student replies that she doesn't understand the assignment. The teacher then assists the student as the rest of the class continues working.

Understanding these four principles of human behavior is a key to your success in the classroom. As you work to fully apply and practice each one, you will feel confident when approaching the classroom because you can make correct decisions about managing behavior. The most important thing to remember about each of these principles is that they are a call to action on your part—you can manage student behavior properly only by first managing **your own.**

Five Skills for Effective Classroom Management

The following skills for guiding student behavior are based on the four principles of human behavior previously discussed. Understanding and effectively using these skills will help prevent unnecessary classroom management problems and prepare you to handle the challenging situations that may occur.

Skill One:	The Ability to Get and Keep Students On Task
Skill Two:	The Ability to Maintain a High Rate of Positive Interactions
Skill Three:	The Ability to Teach Expectations
Skill Four:	The Ability to Respond Non-Coercively to Consequential Behavior
Skill Five:	The Ability to Avoid Becoming Trapped

SKILL ONE:
The Ability to Get and Keep Students On Task

Students cannot learn if they are not actively engaged in learning activities—often called being "on task." When students are on task, they will learn more and create fewer classroom management problems. You can help students get and stay on task by remembering these two strategies:

1. Begin instruction or activities immediately.
2. Manage student behavior by walking around.

Note:

Starting the Day
- *Greet students at the door.*
- *Direct students to a starter activity.*
- *Take attendance based on the seating chart while students are working.*
- *Introduce yourself as the teacher.*
- *Proceed with the written lesson plan.*

For additional downloads, visit:
STEDI.org/ Handbook

Begin Instruction or Activities Immediately

The sooner you get students on task, the easier it is to keep them actively engaged in constructive activities. Work to minimize the time you spend on responsibilities like taking roll and lunch count. Dragging things out at the start of class simply provides time for students to get bored and start behaving inappropriately. One way to get students immediately on task is to greet the students at the door and direct them to a starter activity.

Some permanent teachers may leave instructions for a starter activity to be completed at the beginning of class. If such an activity is not outlined in the lesson plan, prepare an activity that students can work on as soon as they walk into the classroom.

IDEAS FOR STARTER ACTIVITIES

Many effective substitute teachers start the day by having students make name tags, help construct a seating chart (if one was not left), write in a student journal or engage in silent reading. For more ideas, visit **STEDI.org/Handbook**

Starter activities serve three purposes in the classroom:
1. Having a starter activity sets a professional tone for the day.
2. Starter activities get students actively engaged in a learning activity immediately, which helps discourage inappropriate behavior.
3. Starter activities give you time to take roll and prepare materials for a smooth transition to the next activity.

After students have had time to complete the starter activity, tell them the schedule of activities for the rest of the day (or have it written on the board). Now is the time to quickly review expectations, explain consequences, and introduce any incentives or early-finisher activities you will be using. Share any information left by the permanent teacher about what they should accomplish during the day, and then get students involved in the next learning activity as quickly as possible.

NAME TAGS

Name tags are a tremendous help when you're directing class discussions and managing student behavior. Have students make one out of commercial name tags, adhesive file folder labels, or strips of masking tape. They can be worn or kept on students' desks throughout the day.

SEATING CHART

A seating chart is a valuable tool you can use to take roll and call students by name. Sometimes you may not be able to locate a seating chart, or the seating chart left by the permanent teacher may not be current. If this is the case, you can quickly make a seating chart by using small sticky notes and a file folder from your **SubPack** (see more, page 76). Distribute a sticky note to each student, and have them write their name on it. Then, arrange the names on the file folder in the same configuration as the desks in the classroom. The few minutes it takes to establish an accurate seating chart at the beginning of class is well worth the effort.

Note:

When students need to go to the restroom or the library, send only one student at a time. When the first one returns, a second one may go. Be sure to check the school's policy on students moving about the building. Many schools today (especially at the elementary level) use a buddy system so that students are never alone.

MANAGE BY WALKING AROUND

There is a direct relationship between how close a teacher is to students and how well students behave. The easiest and most effective strategy for keeping students on task is for the teacher to walk around the classroom in a random pattern. Wear comfortable shoes and plan to be on your feet all day monitoring, assisting, providing positive reinforcement, and using proximity (nearness to students), to keep them on task.

Do not underestimate the power of the proximity strategy; you will be amazed at how many undesirable behavior problems will be taken care of just by placing yourself nearer to a student. In most cases, it will not be required to talk to the student who is behaving inappropriately. Instead, focus on reinforcing on-task behavior with verbal praise.

Also, don't forget that the teacher should be the most on-task person in the classroom. By walking around the classroom, instead of reading a book at the permanent teacher's desk, you are modeling the on-task classroom behavior you want students to follow.

STAY ON TASK YOURSELF

Do not allow yourself to be led off task by student protests and long, useless discussions. If students complain, respond with empathy, understanding, and firmness. Don't, however, compromise your expectations or waste instructional time by being overly sympathetic.

Example: Students getting the teacher off task

Teacher:	*"Please take out your reading books and read silently at your desk for the next 20 minutes."*
Students:	*"Reading is boring. We never read before lunch time."*
Teacher:	*"You know, when I was your age, I also thought reading was boring. Sometimes I used to just sit at my desk, hold my book open, and pretend to read. Have any of you ever done anything like that?"*
Student:	*"Well, last year I did that one time. But it was still really boring..." etc.*

Example: Teacher getting the students back on task

Teacher:	*"Please take out your reading books and read silently at your desk for the next 20 minutes."*
Students:	*"Reading is boring. We never read before lunch time."*
Teacher:	*"You know, I hear you, it's hard to have a schedule thrown off. When I was your age, sometimes I also thought reading was boring, but that's what we need to do before lunch."*

Other On-Task Strategies

Sometimes an event outside the classroom, such as an assembly, fire drill, or rousing game of soccer at recess makes it difficult to get and keep students on task. On other occasions, the entire class may be off task or out of control for no apparent reason. The permanent teacher may use techniques, such as silent signals or prompt/response procedures, that refocus the class. If you see these techniques outlined in the lesson plans or explained by a student, don't hesitate to implement them. If this doesn't work or you don't know what the permanent teacher usually does, the following strategies will get the attention of the entire class.

REFOCUSING THE CLASS STRATEGY ONE:
Captivate and Redirect

Often the best way to deal with major disruptions is to minimize the event by capturing and redirecting students' attention. For example, have students complete an activity that requires mental concentration (activity ideas can be found in Chapter Six and online at STEDI.org/Handbook). Involving students in an engaging and mentally challenging learning activity will help them settle back down into the routine of the day.

REFOCUSING THE CLASS STRATEGY TWO:
Whisper

Your first instinct in a situation where the entire class is noisy and off task may be to raise your voice above the noise level of the room and demand attention. However, when students hear you speak loudly they may assume it is all right for them to raise their voices as well.

A productive strategy is to whisper. Move to the front of the room and begin giving instructions very quietly. As students begin to hear you, they will need to become quiet in order to understand what you are saying. Soon students who are still inattentive will also focus and listen to the instructions. When you have the attention of the entire class, you can then give instructions or directions as needed.

REFOCUSING THE CLASS STRATEGY THREE:
Write and Erase

If students are between activities and talking among themselves, one way to get their attention and give further instructions is to begin writing and erasing the instructions on the board, one word at a time. For example, if you wanted them to get their science books out of their desks, you would write the word *"Get"* on the whiteboard and then erase it. You would next write the word *"your"* and erase it. Then, write *"science"* and erase it, etc. Students soon become involved in trying to figure out what you are writing and realize that they are missing the instructions. You will quickly have the undivided attention of the entire class.

What are other ways you've seen teachers refocus students to get them back on task?

Note:

When erasing a board, use vertical strokes; your hips will show the least amount of movement. Horizontal strokes make hips shake, which students may find humorous and thus distracting.

STUDENTS IN THE HALLS

- Have a couple of extra pens or pencils with you for students who have "forgotten" theirs and would rather go to their lockers and walk the halls than be in class.

- Try to be in the hall between classes. If the students see a teacher, they are less likely to behave inappropriately. Most bullying incidents happen in the hallways and the bathrooms.

- Always keep students in class for the full amount of time. Never let students go early for lunch or the break unless the permanent teacher or the teacher next door says it is okay. Some schools have very strict rules about the number of students allowed in the cafeteria/hallways at a time.

SKILL TWO:
The Ability to Maintain a
High Rate of Positive Interactions

Positive Teacher-to-Student Interactions

The behavior a teacher gives the most attention to is the behavior that is going to prevail in the classroom. On average, teachers allow 98 percent of all appropriate student behavior to go unrecognized and are two to three times more likely to recognize inappropriate behavior. If you spend your time as a substitute teacher reacting to and reinforcing only undesirable behavior, you will find that students continue that pattern.

Rather than trying to weaken undesirable behavior using adverse or negative processes, research has shown that strengthening desirable behavior through positive reinforcement does more to make a classroom favorable to learning than any other skill.

Note:

Dr. Ben Bissell has outlined five conditions of praise. We don't want to make students into what researchers call *"praise junkies,"* but it is important to let students know when they have met the expectations.

- **Praise must be authentic.** We need to praise people for actions that we genuinely appreciate.
- **Praise must be specific.** Praise a specific action rather than giving the student a general *"good job."*
- **Praise needs to be immediate.**
- **Praise must be clean.** This means that you should praise a behavior for no other reason than to express your gratitude. You can't have other motives. More importantly, it also means that praise can't include a *"however"* statement. For example, *"Thank you for working on your assignment, you got 100%, but you didn't stop talking the entire time."*
- **Praise needs to be private.** This means that the act of praising a student shouldn't cause any embarrassment—when praise is embarrassing, it becomes coercive.

Quoted in What Great Teachers Do Differently by Dr. Todd Whitaker. Originally given in a paper called The Paradoxical Leader by Dr. Benjamin Bissell in 1992.

In general, positive verbal praise, a smile or nod, and other appropriate gestures, are among the very best ways to interact in a positive manner with students. Negative and corrective interactions should be outnumbered by positive interactions, with a recommended ratio of **one negative** (or corrective) interaction to **eight positive** interactions.

It can be difficult to remain positive in challenging classroom situations. One way to prepare for this is to determine situations in which you are most inclined to be negative by filling out the **Anticipate a Problem** form (see page 37). This form will help you anticipate how you will respond to inappropriate behavior in the classroom. Remember that you are learning a new skill, which needs to be practiced several times in order for it to feel natural.

At times, situations will arise that will be so annoying and unnerving that every positive interaction you have ever practiced will completely escape your recollection. When you can't think of an appropriate way to respond and feel overwhelmed with the urge to react in a negative manner, don't do anything! Unless what you are about to say or do has a high probability for making things better, it is better to do nothing at all.

Remember:
The behavior you are trying to control is your own.

For additional downloads, visit: **STEDI.org/ Handbook**

POSITIVE INTERACTION STRATEGY ONE:
The Designated Problem Student

On occasion, a teacher may leave a note about a problem student, or a neighboring teacher may warn you about a troublemaker. In this case, you can often prevent potential problems by being proactive and positive.

When the students arrive, identify the student and request that she be a helper for the day. Ask for assistance with special jobs that keep her positively occupied. Be positive in your interactions and thank her for assisting.

> How can you adapt this strategy to fit a middle or high school setting?

POSITIVE INTERACTION STRATEGY TWO:
"You vs. Them"

Sometimes you may get the feeling that the whole class, or at least several students, have secretly planned to make the day as difficult for you as possible. Most "You vs. Them" scenarios turn out to be a lose-lose situation for everyone involved.

You might try an activity from the **Five-Minute Filler section on page 111.** Interact with the students early in the day—let them get to know you better and see that you have a sense of humor. Chances are, once you break the ice and establish rapport with the students, the remainder of the day will go more smoothly. Making the classroom a battleground for control will usually make things worse.

Risk-Free Student Response Opportunities

A risk-free learning environment is one where students are not afraid to respond—an environment that is free of failure and criticism. As you provide opportunities for students to give correct responses, you are also setting up opportunities to positively acknowledge these successes. Student response opportunities and active participation in the learning process play an important role in student achievement. Allowing students to share openly and participate directly in activities is an important part of the learning process and also cuts down on inappropriate behavior. When students are engaged in appropriate responses to learning activities, they have neither the inclination nor the time to be engaged in inappropriate behavior. Try to lecture as little as possible and involve students through questions instead. Provide opportunities for risk-free student responses immediately. Let students answer questions that illustrate or explain the point you are trying to get across.

Be sure to give all a chance to respond and ask questions. There are always students who continually raise their hands, anxious to say just about anything. On the other hand, there are also those students who sit in class, never asking a question or making a comment. Instead of slipping into the habit of calling on only those students who are most attentive and willing to answer, try placing the names of all the students in a container and drawing them out randomly. Make sure to put each name back in the container, otherwise students who have already responded will lose interest.

Here are some tips for how to create risk-free response opportunities:
- Ask the student to repeat what has been said.
- Call on students who you think know the answer.
- Ask students to respond to questions by writing answers on a piece of paper.
- Have students answer in pairs or small groups (limit students to 30-second discussions).
- Remember that not all information has to pass through you.

HANDLING WRONG ANSWERS:
Echo the Correct Response

Suppose you asked a question expecting a correct response, but for whatever reason the student didn't give the right answer. In such situations, don't dwell on the failure of the student or the incorrect answer. Instead, direct the question and the class' attention to another student who you think knows the answer. Once the question has been answered correctly, come back to the original student and ask the question again, allowing her to echo the correct response. This makes the experience a success for the student.

EXAMPLE

Teacher:	*"Jenni, how do you spell the word 'symphony'?"*
Jenni:	*"S - Y - M - F - O - N - Y"*
Teacher:	*"Very good, Jenni. You are very close. Is there any one else that thinks they know how you spell symphony? Gabe, why don't you give it a try?"*
Gabe:	*"S - Y - M - P - H - O - N - Y"*
Teacher:	*"That is correct. Good job, Gabe. Jenni, will you please spell symphony again?"*
Jenni:	*"S - Y - M - P - H - O - N - Y"*
Teacher:	*"Very good! That is exactly right."*

Occasionally, students will respond inaccurately or inappropriately on purpose. Do not allow yourself to be drawn off target and into their control. Even though the student response was inappropriate, it is inconsequential and can be ignored. Move on to a student who is likely to respond correctly and appropriately. Provide positive reinforcement for the correct response and then continue with the discussion. Responding to the inappropriate comment will most likely reinforce the behavior and prompt other unhelpful responses.

SKILL THREE:
The Ability to Teach Expectations

Teaching expectations should provide boundaries and establish standards for student success.

Types of expectations include:
- Classroom Expectations—Rules
- Instructional Expectations
- Procedural Expectations

As a substitute teacher, your first objective should be to model the expectations of the permanent teacher. Try to determine the classroom rules and strategies used by the permanent teacher to get the attention of the class. These may be in the lesson plans or posted somewhere in the classroom. You can also ask students about the procedures they are used to. Be sure to find out the permanent teacher's expectations about mp3 players and cell phones and follow them, even if you don't agree. Be prepared to set your own expectations if you can't figure out what the permanent teacher usually does.

Class expectations should be clear, concise, and give specific instructions for student behavior. Phrases such as *"be cooperative," "respect others,"* and *"be polite and helpful"* are too general and take too much time to explain. Effective expectations such as *"Follow directions the first time they are given,"* are direct, provide specific standards, and are appropriate for any grade level. The number of expectations should correlate with the age and ability of the students; in general, limit them to five or less.

Note:

One way to make general expectations more specific is to inform students what your expectation looks like. For example, we could take the common expectation "be respectful" and change it to "Respect yourself by doing your best work and removing negative language about yourself from your vocabulary."

Or "Respect others by looking at them when they speak, express appreciation for their contributions, and only speak kind words to one another."

Or "Respect school property by returning borrowed materials and leaving the classroom materials in an orderly fashion."

Once classroom expectations have been taught they should be displayed somewhere in the room. If the permanent teacher has not already posted them, you can write them on the board or on a poster-sized sheet of paper you carry in your **SubPack**. In primary grades, using pictures in addition to words is a good way to convey your expectations.

Each assignment and activity throughout the day will have its own set of instructional and procedural expectations. As you develop and explain these expectations, realize that students need four things in order to successfully meet the expectations you establish:

1. They need to know exactly what it is they are supposed to do.
2. They need to know how they are expected to do it.
3. They need to have the necessary tools to accomplish the expected task.
4. They need to know exactly how much time they have to complete the task.

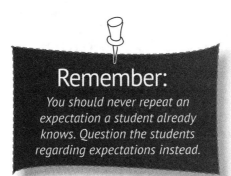

Remember:

You should never repeat an expectation a student already knows. Question the students regarding expectations instead.

EXAMPLE

Teacher: *"When I say begin, stop reading and quietly put your reading book away. Get out your math book and paper. Open the book to page 112. You have one minute to do this. Please begin."*

Explaining instructional and procedural expectations in the form of a step-by-step process often makes it easier for students to remember the expectations and complete the corresponding task appropriately. Just telling students what your expectations are is often not enough. Expectations should be explained, restated by the students, demonstrated, and even role-played until you are sure the students understand what is expected of them.

Questioning students helps you know if everyone understands and remembers the expectations. You can have students respond as an entire group and act out behaviors, such as raising their hands, which requires every student in the class to understand and acknowledge the expectation.

MINIMIZING TIME DURING TRANSITIONS

When students are transitioning from one activity to another it is easy for them to get off task. Consider ways that you can minimize transition time; following are a few ideas:

- Hand out the worksheets or materials while students are working on a previous assignment.
- Set materials out for easier access.
- While students are working, write instructional and procedural expectations for the next activity on the board for quick reference.

What other ways can you think of to minimize transition time?

For additional downloads, visit:

STEDI.org/ Handbook

Have Students Restate Expectations

Having students restate expectations is one way to ensure that students understand your expectations. The few minutes it takes to communicate expectations for each activity is well worth the time to prevent inappropriate behavior. Once you have established your expectations, stick with them! Firmness, fairness, and consistency are the keys to classroom management. Praising students when expectations are met reinforces appropriate behavior.

EXAMPLE

Teacher:	*(Calling on attentive student) "Robbie, thank you for paying attention. What do I expect you to do when you want to answer a question or say something?"*
Robbie:	*"You want me to raise my hand."*
Teacher:	*"That's right, Robbie. I expect you to raise your hand."*

Having students restate expectations is also a great way to find out a permanent teacher's expectations.

EXAMPLE

Teacher:	*"Ella, what is your teacher's expectation when it comes to cell phones?"*
Ella:	*"He lets us use them whenever we want."*
Teacher:	*(Without hesitation) "Max, what is your teacher's expectation when it comes to cell phones?"*
Max:	*"We can use them whenever we want."*
Teacher:	*(Without hesitation) "Rana, What is your teacher's expectation when it comes to cell phones?"*
Rana:	*"They can't be out during class."*
Teacher:	*"Max, Ella, what is you teacher's expectation when it comes to cell phones?"*
Max, Ella:	*"They can't be out during class."*
Teacher:	*"That's right, thank you. It is the same for today as well. Thank you to those who have their cell phones put away and are ready for the next activity."*

In this example, the students know exactly what expectations are set, and they can then teach each other. Later in the class if a student has her cell phone out, you can privately ask her what the expectation is and trust that she knows it, because you took extra time to clarify the rule at the beginning of class.

Note:

It is your responsibility to know and understand each school's policy for electronic devices so you can be consistent. Also note that you need to set an example for the class by following the same policies yourself.

SKILL FOUR:
The Ability to Respond Non-Coercively
to Consequential Behavior

Any time a student behaves inappropriately you will probably find it annoying. However, the type of behavior, rather than the annoyance level, should be your guide for implementing an appropriate teacher response strategy. Inappropriate student behaviors can be classified as either consequential or inconsequential.

Consequential behaviors are those that have a significant negative effect on the learning environment and interfere with the rights of other students to learn.

Inconsequential behaviors are those that the classroom environment would be better off without, but their negative impact on student learning is minimal. Inconsequential behaviors, such as tapping your pencil on the desk, can become consequential if they escalate or persist over a period of time.

Ignore Inconsequential Behavior

Most inappropriate student behavior—roughly 94%—is inconsequential, regardless of how annoying it is. A substitute teacher responding, whether verbally or through body language, to inconsequential student behavior, is providing reinforcement and the frequency of these behaviors will likely increase.

A better approach is to ignore inconsequential behavior and respond positively to appropriate behavior with a smile, verbal praise, a nod, or other appropriate gestures.

EXAMPLE

When asking a question of the class, a student responds without raising his hand for permission to speak or speaks out of turn.

Step One: Do not respond to the disruptive student. Look at those who are raising their hands and call on one of them saying, *"Thank you for raising your hand,"* then allow her to answer the question.

Step Two: If the student continues to speak without raising his hand when you ask the next question, continue to reinforce the students who are behaving appropriately, and using the proximity strategy, move closer to the student who is not cooperating.

Generally after steps one and two, a noncompliant student will cooperate and the inappropriate behavior will have stopped. It is important to quickly recognize and reinforce the appropriate behavior of students as they comply with expectations.

Respond Non-Coercively to Consequential Behavior

While most student behavior is inconsequential, there are inappropriate student behaviors that are of consequence and need to be addressed. Consequential behavior can be defined as behavior that is:

a. Persistent and disruptive.
b. Destructive to the learning environment.
c. Physically or verbally abusive.

Teachers commonly respond to consequential behavior using coercion. Coercion involves attempts to achieve compliance through the use of threats or force. The intent is to compel students to behave out of fear of what will happen to them if they do not. Coercion makes a student want to escape or avoid the coercer; it does nothing to address the problem.

At best, coercion instills a sense of fear in students that prevents them from acting out. While on the surface the problem seems to have gone away, in reality you have threatened the student's self-confidence and destroyed the risk-free atmosphere.

For example, some teachers use sarcasm to make students comply. They do this by making fun of or talking down to the student in front of peers. While this type of negative teacher behavior may look like it works, it is destroying the student's confidence, and any rapport the teacher may have established with that student is ruined.

When responding to consequential behavior the pattern that should be followed is to stop the inappropriate behavior and redirect the student to an appropriate behavior—which is typically back on task.

REINFORCE APPROPRIATE BEHAVIOR

Believe it or not, frequent teacher attention in the form of praise is more effective in increasing appropriate behavior than reprimands. Simple phrases such as, *"Thank you for raising your hand, Andrew,"* and *"I appreciate that Jose, Su-Ling, and Monica followed my directions so quickly,"* are great positive motivators. You can also try using tangible rewards, such as points or tickets, to encourage appropriate behavior.

By overlooking inconsequential off-task behaviors and giving attention to students who are meeting expectations, you are creating a positive classroom atmosphere where all students have a reason to behave appropriately.

REDIRECT STUDENT BEHAVIOR

Instead of being coercive, a better way to handle consequential behavior is to stop the student behavior, then redirect it. This should be done as privately and quietly as possible. The following are six steps for stopping and redirecting inappropriate student behavior:

1. Say something positive to the student or class.
2. Briefly describe the problem behavior.
3. Describe the desired alternative behavior.
4. Give a reason why the new behavior is more desirable.
5. Check for understanding.
6. Provide positive feedback.

EXAMPLE

1. Say something positive.	*"Isabella, I enjoy having you in class. You have a lot of very creative ideas."*
2. Describe the problem behavior.	*"Just then when I asked you to stop talking to Adam and read your book, you continued to talk to him."*
3. Describe the desired behavior. *follow my instructions immediately."*	*"When I ask you to do something, I need you to*
4. Give a reason the new behavior is desirable.	*"If you will stop talking to Adam, the class will be quieter and everyone, including you, will be able to finish the reading task more quickly."*
5. Check for understanding.	*"Isabella, what should you do when I give you instructions?"* (Isabella says, *"Do it."*) If Isabella does not respond, prompt her. If she responds inappropriately, repeat the question without displaying anger.
6. Provide positive feedback.	When Isabella responds correctly, the teacher says, *"Great! This time you picked up your book and started reading. Well done!"*

This process can take less than two minutes and becomes quite natural when you practice it regularly. At this point you might be thinking, *"Well that's all right for young students, but not for the kids I work with."* However, this strategy was developed at Boys Town in Omaha, Nebraska, and has been shown to be successful with students of all ages, including high school.

REEVALUATE THE SITUATION

One of the first steps you should take when a student or group of students is behaving inappropriately is to reevaluate the situation. If a group of students will not stop talking, step back and see if you can figure out why they are talking. Perhaps they do not understand the assignment and need more instruction from you, or you could even restructure the assignment to allow students to work in small groups.

USE PROXIMITY

Proximity is an easy-to-use strategy for dealing with many inappropriate behaviors. If a student or group of students is off task or disrupting the class, move closer in incremental steps. As you move toward the problem, behavior will often change, and students will comply with expectations without having to say a word.

RESTATE EXPECTATIONS

Sometimes students are off task because they do not fully understand your expectations or the related consequences. Start by restating the expectations and the positive motivators or consequences. Then question students to see if they understand. Sometimes this is all it takes to get a class back on task.

EXAMPLE

Teacher: *"It is important for everyone to follow the instructions that were given. Please listen carefully as I restate what we need to be doing. You should be working individually on this assignment; we will have a few minutes at the end of class to participate in a group activity. But for now each of you should be working silently on your math worksheet. You have 15 more minutes. If you have a question or need help, please raise your hand and I will come to your desk.*

I want to make sure that you understand the expectations, so I will be watching for everyone to work silently in the next 10 seconds. Once I see you working, I can start walking around giving tickets to those who are on task."

STATE THE FACTS

In some situations, stating the facts motivates students to behave appropriately. For example, if you suspect students aren't sitting in the right seats, tell them that you are writing a list, based on the seating chart, that you will leave for the permanent teacher of students who are working and on task.

EXAMPLE

Teacher: *"I know it's a lot of work to get done, but it's what your teacher left for us to accomplish today."*

ACKNOWLEDGE AND RESTATE

Some students may vocally express negative opinions, inappropriate views, and frustrations. Verbally acknowledging a student's comment validates him as a person and often diffuses an emotionally charged situation. Phrases such as *"I can tell that you…"* or *"It is obvious that…"* can be used to acknowledge what the student said without getting emotionally involved yourself. Transition words such as *"however"* and *"nevertheless"* bring the dialogue back to restating the expected behavior.

> **EXAMPLE**
>
> **Teacher:** *"I can see you are not very interested in this topic, but I need you to construct a timeline for the industrial revolution. It needs to be done by the end of class, so I'll come check on you in a minute or two to see how you're doing."*

USE THE "I UNDERSTAND" METHOD

There are two words that can stop most protests from any student and let you take control of the situation. These words are *"I understand."* If a student says, *"But that's not fair!"* you can say, *"I understand that is how you feel, however, these are the expectations for today."* If a student says, *"You're a terrible sub!"* you can say, *"I understand you feel that way, however, I am the teacher today and you are expected to follow my directions."* If a student says, *"This assignment is stupid,"* you can say, *"I hear you, but you will need to have it completed for class tomorrow."*

REMOVE, IDENTIFY, AND REDIRECT

In some instances, it is best to remove the student from the situation before addressing the behavior. Since you need to continually supervise all of the students in the class, removing the student should take him out of earshot, but still allow you to watch the rest of the class. Calmly ask the student to go to the back of the room or into the doorway. Direct the class to resume working, and then approach the student.

Stay calm and in control of the situation and explain to the students what expectation was broken. Then, explain what the consequence will be if she continues to act inappropriately. Make sure to express your confidence that he can correct the behavior and have the student restate what is expected.

For additional downloads, visit: **STEDI.org/ Handbook**

 ## USE ASSERTIVE STATEMENTS

Be assertive so students don't feel they can manipulate your decisions and authority. Giving instructive statements that also assert what students need to do is a great way to show what you expect from them.

- *"Thanks to those who have their reading books out, I will need you to read for the next 10 minutes."*
- *"Wow, I'm impressed with how many are lined up ready to go. Once everyone is in line, the line leader can then lead us down the hallway."*
- *"I'm watching for everyone to have their names on their paper so we can begin."*

 ## ESTABLISH CONSEQUENCES

Many times you will teach in classrooms where the permanent teacher has already established consequences for inappropriate behavior. Using these established consequences helps maintain consistency for students and saves you from having to develop consequences of your own. In situations where you do have to devise and implement consequences, keep the following in mind:

- When possible, consequences should be a natural outcome or directly related to the behavior. For example, if a student is off task and does not finish her assignment, the consequence could be that she has to continue working on her assignment while the rest of the class is participating in a fun activity.
- Consequences and how to enforce them should not give extra attention to misbehaving students.
- A negative consequence for one student may be reinforcing to another. If the consequence does not change the behavior in time, change the consequence (see the Fourth Principle of Human Behavior on page 4).
- Consequences should be administered quickly and quietly without getting emotionally involved.
- All consequences should be reasonable, appropriate, and in accordance with district or school guidelines and policies.

Students need to know, **in advance**, what they can expect as a result of their behavior (both positive and negative) so they can make informed choices about how to behave. In other words, you should avoid springing new consequences on students out of nowhere after the behavior has already taken place. Consequences should also be communicated to students as predetermined outcomes of behavior rather than threats. It is a good idea to discuss consequences when you are explaining expectations for the classroom or a particular activity.

Remember:

Assign consequences at an individual student level rather than punishing the whole group. Punishing the entire class for the misbehavior of one student usually results in two negative outcomes. First, the student receives a lot of attention as he is singled out and recognized as the cause for the class consequences. Second, any trust you had established with the remaining students is lost because it feels unfair. Instead, correct the behavior and apply the consequences for that individual student, which will avoid giving him unneeded attention for his negative behavior.

EXAMPLE

Teacher:	*"During today's science lesson, you will be using water and working with syringes at your desk. I expect you to use the syringes, water, and other materials appropriately as outlined in the activity. Anyone who uses these materials inappropriately will be asked to leave their group and observe the remainder of the activity in a seat away from the lab area."*
Teacher:	*"Jordan, what is it that I expect during this activity?"*
Jordan:	*"To use the syringes, water, and other materials correctly as outlined in the activity."*
Teacher:	*"Shelley, what are the benefits of using these materials correctly?"*
Shelley:	*"I can remain with my group and complete the activity."*
Teacher:	*"That is right. What will be the consequences if someone uses the materials inappropriately, Tyrel?"*
Tyrel:	*"He will be asked to leave the group and watch the rest of the activity from a seat away from the lab area."*

For additional downloads, visit:
STEDI.org/ Handbook

MANAGE PROBLEMS INSIDE THE CLASSROOM

The following advice comes from a former elementary school principal:

Effective substitute teachers gain more respect from students when they handle behavior problems in the classroom. Be careful of the message that you might be conveying when you send students to the principal's office. Of course, students engaged in any behavior that affects student safety, such as fighting, should be sent to the principal's office.

Classroom management is ongoing and never ends. Arrive early so that you will be organized, informed about the classroom and prepared for the students. The following points will help you with your classroom management skills as you deal with behavior problems in the classroom.

- Take charge and be confident.
- State expectations and rules.
- Establish logical consequences.
- Be consistent—follow through with what you say you are going to do.
- Respond firmly and respectfully to students.
- Consult with team members and the principal about the class and any particular classroom management methods that may have been successful in the past.

If you cannot find the permanent teacher's rules, expectations, and consequences, be prepared with your own. Four to five rules that are simple, specific, clear, and stated positively are generally all that are needed to have a well-managed classroom. Consequences should be for both appropriate and inappropriate behavior.

Some schools have school-wide behavior plans. Be sure to ask at each school and be prepared to follow the plan prior to entering the classroom.

Submitted by Linda Robinson from Loudoun County Public Schools, VA

Responding Non-Coercively to a Refusal to Do Work

In some classrooms you may have a student or students who refuse to complete an assignment or participate in activities. Your first response should be recognition of students who are on task and positive encouragement for the noncompliant student. If, after you encourage the student to complete the assignment, she makes a statement such as, *"You can't make me,"* an appropriate strategy would be to acknowledge and restate. Disarm the student by acknowledging that she is correct, you cannot force her, and then restate your expectations and consequences if they are not met.

EXAMPLE

Teacher: *"You're right, Daniela, I can't make you complete this task. I can, however, expect you to have it completed before you leave for lunch. If it is not finished by then, you will have to take it home and work on it. I also expect you to remain quiet and not disrupt the other students who are choosing to complete the assignment at this time."*

It is important to note that many times students may refuse to work simply because they don't understand the task. Students would rather appear bad than stupid. If this is the case, you may need to restate the concept or provide extra help for the student. You can also emphasize what the student can do or has already accomplished and recognize student effort.

Responding Non-Coercively to Inappropriate Language or Derogatory Remarks

Occasionally, a student may use obscene language or make a derogatory remark about you, another student, or the permanent teacher. Avoid taking the remarks personally, respond to the behavior in a professional manner and don't let your emotions override your behavior management skills. The classroom expectations and consequences established at the beginning of the day have provisions for dealing with this challenging situation—implement them! You might say something such as, *"Ben, you chose to break the classroom rule regarding using proper language. What is the consequence?"*

Do not ask the student why he said what he did—just acknowledge that he chose to break a rule or behave inappropriately. Dismiss the incident as quickly as possible and resume class work. Have the student repeat the consequence and then carry it out. Put the incident out of your mind as quickly as possible and resume class work with a pleasant and cheerful tone in your voice.

Responding Non-Coercively to a Fight

If you see two students yelling at each other or poised for a fight, make sure to respond quickly and decisively. Do not hesitate to get help from another teacher if needed. Aggressive behavior can usually be extinguished by a firm command as you move toward the problem saying, *"Stop right now and take a seat quietly against the wall."* Students will most likely respond to your calm, authoritative voice combined with an instructive statement. Try to end verbal disagreements and name-calling early, so that things don't escalate into pushing or fighting.

If students are engaged physically, you must act quickly and with authority. Tell them to step back away from each other immediately. Do not get angry, excited, or show a lot of emotion—because this can inflame an already tense situation. Do not place yourself between students to try to stop the engagement, as this can be very dangerous for you. Instead focus on giving clear instructions and send for help.

Responding Non-Coercively to Threats

Threats are difficult to handle—the best strategy varies with each situation. However, should a student threaten you or another student, the most important thing to do is stay calm and emotionally detached so you can evaluate and manage the situation professionally. The school may have a policy on how to handle such situations and you may want to ask a neighboring teacher about how to be prepared.

THREAT STRATEGY ONE:
Acknowledge and Redirect

A threat is often the result of an emotional response. Ignoring the student will probably evoke more threats and perhaps even aggression. Responding with threats of your own may accelerate the confrontation. Instead, acknowledge the threat calmly and direct the student to begin something constructive.

If you feel that more discussion is needed, it is often wise to wait until after the lesson, later in the day, or to refer the student to a school counselor so that the emotional distance can help them have a clearer perspective.

EXAMPLE

Teacher: *"I understand that you are very angry right now. However, I need you to sit down and begin completing page 112 in your math book. We will discuss the situation after lunch."*

THREAT STRATEGY TWO:
Get Help!

If you feel that you or any of the students are in danger of physical harm, stay calm and immediately call or send someone to the office to get help. After help has arrived and the situation is under control, document the event by recording what happened prior to the threat, what you said and did, what the student said and did, as well as the actions of anyone else involved in the situation.

Note:

Students with weapons or a knife of any kind should be immediately reported. If you suspect this problem, contact the office for further help.

SKILL FIVE:
The Ability to Avoid Becoming Trapped

Teachers, including substitute teachers, often find themselves caught in one of the following seven discipline traps. If you get caught in these traps, you will lose some of your power as an effective educator. Recognizing and avoiding these traps helps you provide students with a better learning environment and also avoid a lot of classroom management stress.

TRAP ONE:
The Criticism Trap

Students need and respond to attention—and whether this attention reinforces appropriate or inappropriate behavior is up to you. The criticism trap comes from paying too much attention to negative behavior, which actually highlights and encourages that behavior.

Avoid the criticism trap by reinforcing appropriate behavior instead! Do your best to have at least eight positive interactions for every one negative interaction with a student.

FALLING INTO THE CRITICISM TRAP:

Teacher: *"This generation, all you can do is listen to your mp3 players and text on your cell phones. You have no consideration for people in the same room as yourself."*

AVOIDING THE CRITICISM TRAP:

Teacher: *"I'm impressed with how hard some of you are working. Thank you for keeping cell phones away while you are working; it makes for a better learning environment."*

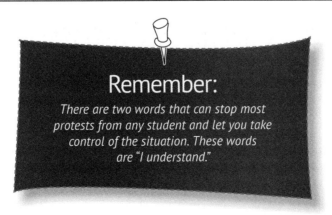

Remember:
There are two words that can stop most protests from any student and let you take control of the situation. These words are "I understand."

TRAP TWO:
The Common Sense Trap

The common sense trap is where common sense, reasoning, or logic is used to try and persuade students to change their behavior. This strategy is ineffective because students don't learn anything new and are not offered a reasonable incentive to change their behavior.

Avoid the common sense trap by creating a positive environment where there are incentives to change and where positive consequences reinforce that change.

FALLING INTO THE COMMON SENSE TRAP:

Teacher: *"Nicki, let's go over this again. As I explained earlier, you should have your assignment completed by the end of class. Look at how much you have left to do. You keep telling me that you will finish in time, but unless you hurry up you never will. It's up to you to get it done. If you don't complete your assignments, you're going to have a lot of homework."*

AVOIDING THE COMMON SENSE TRAP:

Teacher: *"Nicki, you have done the first four problems right. However, I can see that you still have a lot of this assignment left to complete. In order to participate in the end of the day activity, you will need to hurry up and finish your work. I'll be back in a few minutes to see how you are doing."*

TRAP THREE:
The Questioning Trap

There are three reasons why questioning students about inappropriate behavior is usually unproductive.
1. You want students to change the behavior, not just talk about it.
2. One question usually leads to more questions that simply waste learning time.
3. As you question a student about an inappropriate behavior, you are actually calling attention to and reinforcing the behavior you want to eliminate.

Avoid the questioning trap by not asking students about their inappropriate behavior unless you really need the information to redirect the behavior. A better approach is to restate the expected behavior, make sure they understand the expectation, then positively reinforce the expected behavior as was discussed in Skill Four: Responding Non-Coercively to Consequential Behavior (page 1).

FALLING INTO THE QUESTIONING TRAP:

Teacher: *"Why aren't you working on your assignment?"*

Student: *"Because I don't want to."*

Teacher: *"Why don't you want to?"*

Student: *"It's stupid."*

Teacher: *"What's stupid about it?" Etc.*

AVOIDING THE QUESTIONING TRAP:

Teacher: *"What do you need to be working on right now?"*

Student: *"She is talking to me."*

Teacher: *"What do you need to be working on right now?"*

Student: *"My assignment."*

Teacher: *"Thanks for working on that, I'll come back soon and see how you're doing."*

TRAP FOUR:
The Sarcasm Trap

When a teacher resorts to sarcasm by belittling or making fun of students, it destroys the positive classroom environment and may prompt students to lash out with inappropriate remarks of their own. The use of sarcasm suggests that you, as the teacher, do not know any better way of interacting and sets the stage for similar negative interactions between students themselves.

Avoid the sarcasm trap by communicating with students in a positive way. To review maintaining a high ratio of positive interactions, see page 10.

FALLING INTO THE SARCASM TRAP:

Teacher: *"My, my aren't you a smart class? It looks like by age 12 you have all finally learned to find your own seats and sit down after the bell, and to think it only took you half of the morning to do it. I don't know if there is another class in the entire school as smart or quick as you guys."*

AVOIDING THE SARCASM TRAP:

Teacher: *"One of the expectations of this class is to be seated and ready to go to work when the bell rings. I appreciate those of you who were quietly seated when the bell rang today."*

TRAP FIVE:
The Despair and Pleading Trap

There will be days when nothing you do seems to work. As tempting as it may be to confide your feelings of inadequacy and frustration to the students and plead for their help in solving the problem, don't do it! Teachers often become their own worst enemies when they communicate to students that they feel incapable of managing the classroom, and often the inappropriate behavior will accelerate rather than diminish.

Avoid the despair and pleading trap by having a good offense. Come to the classroom prepared with several classroom management strategies. For some classes, positive verbal reinforcement will be enough. In others, you may need to introduce tangible reinforcers such as point systems, end of the day drawings, or special awards (see page 78 for ideas). When you find that one strategy is not working with an individual or class, don't be afraid to try something else.

FALLING INTO THE DESPAIR AND PLEADING TRAP:

Teacher: *(With a distraught expression and hopeless voice) "Come on, class, can't you do me a favor and just be quiet for the rest of class? I've tried everything I know to get you to behave and nothing has worked. What do you think I should do? How can I get you to be quiet?"*

Student: *"Don't ask me, you're the teacher!"*

AVOIDING THE DESPAIR AND PLEADING TRAP:

Teacher: *"Between now and the end of class, I am going to be awarding points to groups who follow my instructions and are on task. At the end of class, the group with the most points will get to choose a reward."*

TRAP SIX:
The Threat Trap

When teachers resort to making threats, they are just one step beyond despair and pleading on the scale of helplessness and the majority of threats are either unreasonable or unenforceable. If you fall into this trap out of frustration, you are communicating to students that you are at a loss of what to do.

Avoid the threat trap by planning ahead. The best way to avoid frustrating situations is to formulate and state both expectations and appropriate consequences in advance. Then reinforce appropriate student behavior and follow through with consequences.

FALLING INTO THE THREAT TRAP:

Teacher: *"If you don't sit down and be quiet right this minute, I'm going to call your parents and have them come and sit next to you for the rest of class!"*

AVOIDING THE THREAT TRAP:

Teacher: *"During this group activity, you are expected to remain in your seat and work quietly with other group members. Should you choose not to do this, you will not be allowed to participate with your group in the review game at the end of the activity."* Wait several minutes for students to comply. *"The members of group number three are doing an excellent job of staying in their seats and working quietly."*

For additional downloads, visit:
STEDI.org/ Handbook

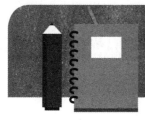

TRAP SEVEN:
The Physical and Verbal Force Trap

The use of physical or verbal force is absolutely inappropriate. Physical force as a behavior management tool is not only unproductive and inappropriate—in many states it is also illegal.

Avoid the physical and verbal force trap by concentrating on restating the expectations in a proactive way. Then, have the student restate and demonstrate the expectation. Keep your cool, count to ten, walk to the other side of the room—do whatever it takes to keep from resorting to force.

FALLING INTO THE PHYSICAL AND VERBAL FORCE TRAP:

Teacher: *"I told you to sit down." Teacher pushes student into her desk. "Now stay there until class is over."*

AVOIDING THE PHYSICAL AND VERBAL FORCE TRAP:

Teacher: *"Right now I need you to sit down and work on your assignment. After I see you working, then we can discuss what the problem is."*

THE SEVEN TRAPS CONCLUSION

The use of any trap-related management strategy is evidence of an unprofessional and unproductive attempt at managing student behavior. These traps can be deceiving because, while they may seem to produce changes in behavior, over time they are certain to backfire and result in the steady deterioration of the positive classroom environment. Be patient and persistent in removing these negative strategies from your classroom interactions.

CLASSROOM MANAGEMENT SUMMARY

By gaining an understanding of basic human behavior and consistently applying the skills discussed in this chapter, you will be better prepared to more effectively manage the behavior of students in the classroom. Reviewing this chapter often will assist you as you continue to develop and expand your repertoire of classroom and behavior management skills.

ADVICE FROM STUDENTS

- Trust us.
- Be fair to everyone.
- Punish only the troublemakers.
- Make learning fun.
- Give us our assignment and let us go to work.
- Allow study time in class.
- Show concern and be willing to help with assignments.
- If I raise my hand, do not ignore me.
- You can be both strict and nice.
- Do not shout.
- Be straightforward with us.
- Be organized.
- Speak quietly and be patient.
- Give us something to work toward.
- Leave your personal life at home.
- Think positively of every student.
- Speak clearly.
- Be reasonable in your expectations.
- Have a sense of humor.
- Follow through with promises and consequences.

101 WAYS TO SAY "GOOD JOB!"

Teachers are two to three times more likely to recognize inappropriate student behavior over appropriate student behavior. Praise is most powerful when it is specific. Here are a variety of phrases you can use to recognize and reinforce positive behavior, without always saying, *"Good job!"*

1. You've got it made.
2. Super!
3. That's right!
4. That's good!
5. You are very good at that.
6. Good work!
7. Exactly right!
8. You have just about got it.
9. You are doing a good job!
10. That's it!
11. Now you have figured it out.
12. Great!
13. I knew you could do it.
14. Congratulations!
15. Not bad.
16. Keep working on it; you are improving.
17. Now you have it.
18. You are learning fast.
19. Good for you!
20. Couldn't have done it better myself.
21. Beautiful!
22. One more time and you'll have it.
23. That's the right way to do it.
24. You did it that time!
25. You are getting better and better.
26. You are on the right track now.
27. Nice going.
28. You haven't missed a thing.
29. Wow!
30. That's the way.
31. Keep up the good work.
32. Terrific!
33. Nothing can stop you now.
34. That's the way to do it.
35. Sensational!
36. You have got your brain in gear today.
37. That's better.
38. Excellent!
39. That was first–class work.
40. That's the best ever.
41. You have just about mastered that.
42. Perfect!
43. That's better than ever before.
44. Much better!
45. Wonderful!
46. You must have been practicing.
47. You did that very well.
48. Fine!
49. Nice going.
50. Outstanding!
51. Fantastic!
52. Tremendous!
53. Now that's what I call a fine job.
54. That's great.
55. You're really improving.
56. Superb!
57. Good remembering!
58. You have got that down pat.
59. You certainly did well today.
60. Keep it up!
61. Congratulations, you got it right!
62. You did a lot of work today.
63. That's it!
64. Marvelous!
65. I like that.
66. Cool!
67. Way to go.
68. You've got the hang of it!

69. You're doing fine.
70. Good thinking.
71. You are learning a lot.
72. Good going.
73. I've never seen anyone do it better.
74. That's a real work of art.
75. Keep on trying!
76. Good for you!
77. Good job!
78. You remembered!
79. That's really nice.
80. Thanks!
81. What neat work!
82. That's "A" work.
83. That's clever.
84. Very interesting.
85. You make it look easy.
86. Excellent effort.
87. Awesome!
88. That's a good point.
89. Superior work.
90. Nice going.
91. I knew you could do it.
92. That looks like it is going to be a great paper.
93. That's coming along nicely.
94. That's an interesting way of looking at it.
95. Out of sight!
96. It looks like you've put a lot of work into this.
97. Right on!
98. Congratulations, you only missed . . .
99. Super-Duper!
100. It's a classic.
101. I'm impressed!

CLASSROOM MANAGEMENT SUMMARY

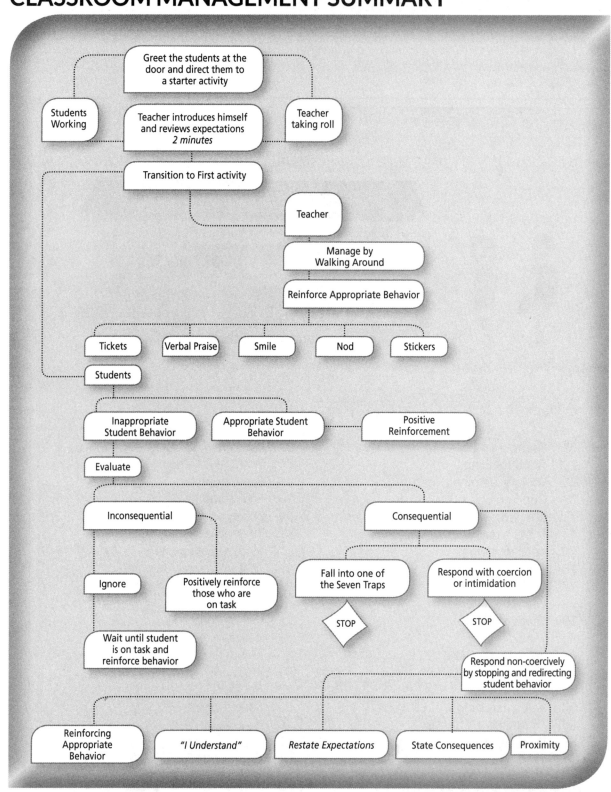

Greet the students at the door and direct them to a starter activity

Students Working

Teacher introduces himself and reviews expectations
2 minutes

Teacher taking roll

Transition to First activity

Teacher

Manage by Walking Around

Reinforce Appropriate Behavior

Tickets | Verbal Praise | Smile | Nod | Stickers

Students

Inappropriate Student Behavior | Appropriate Student Behavior | Positive Reinforcement

Evaluate

Inconsequential | Consequential

Ignore | Positively reinforce those who are on task

Fall into one of the Seven Traps | Respond with coercion or intimidation

STOP | STOP

Wait until student is on task and reinforce behavior

Respond non-coercively by stopping and redirecting student behavior

Reinforcing Appropriate Behavior | *"I Understand"* | *Restate Expectations* | State Consequences | Proximity

ANTICIPATE A PROBLEM FORM

To become more positive and proactive in challenging situations, you must identify and practice positive interaction skills. This form will allow you to anticipate potential problem behaviors and how you can react to that behavior. Remember: the behavior you are trying to control is your own.

ANTICIPATED PROBLEM	POSITIVE, PROACTIVE RESPONSE
I tend to scold or criticize students when they get noisy or out of control.	I'll reinforce a behaving student then look for an opportunity, 30–seconds to a minute later, to verbally reinforce the disruptive student for being on task. I'll re-teach my expectations followed, 30 seconds to a minute later, by verbal praise for being on task.

TEACHING STRATEGIES

*H*ave you ever felt stumped when trying to get students on board during a dry lesson plan or been embarrassed by the sound of crickets when leading a class discussion? Or maybe you've nervously accepted a teaching assignment outside your comfort zone? This chapter is filled with clever tips from the files of experienced teachers to give you just the tools you'll need to get through tough teaching challenges.

In Chapter One, we reviewed five key skills for strong classroom management. A great substitute teacher also needs to guide students through engaging learning activities. **The strategies offered here should complement the lesson, not change or replace the permanent teacher's plan. Remember: substitute teachers should always follow the lesson plan.** However, the instructions may leave room for some creative additions that can add a little life and variety for the students, often cutting down on discipline problems. For example, if the lesson plan includes *"Read chapter four and answer the questions at the end of the chapter,"* you can probably guess students will likely get bored and off task. Try one of the following strategies to help the class stay active and engaged—leading to more student learning and more success (and less headaches!) for you.

These teaching strategies can work for any content area and grade level. They also encourage students to take charge of their own learning, which means you don't need to have prior knowledge of the subject matter in order to lead the activity. The teaching strategies in this chapter are outlined as follows:

Lesson Kickstarters
Brainstorming
KWL Chart

Graphic Organizers
Venn Diagram
Concept Mapping

Questioning Strategies
The Ask, Pause, Call Method
Bloom's Taxonomy for Higher Level Thinking

Group Work Strategies
Cooperative Learning Method
Jigsaw Learning Method

Reviewing Strategies
Smart Art
Invent a Game
Exit Slips

Tip:

Visit STEDI.org/Handbook for downloads of graphic organizers to keep in your **SubPack**.

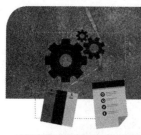

Lesson Kickstarters

Lesson Kickstarters are simple ways to get a lesson into gear. By taking a few minutes on an activity like brainstorming, you give the students a chance to get focused. This ups the chances they will remember what was learned during the lesson.

BRAINSTORMING

Brainstorming is a classic teaching strategy that can be your go-to method for any age group or subject.

How do I lead a productive brainstorming session?

- **Make sure everyone is on the same page.** Have a brief conversation with the students outlining your simple rules for brainstorming. Following are the DOVE rules for brainstorming.

D Don't judge others' ideas—evaluation comes later.

O Original and unconventional ideas are encouraged.

V Volume of ideas—as many as possible in time limit.

E Everyone can participate.

- **Set a time limit.** One to three minutes is usually about right; occasionally up to five minutes might be needed. It is better to start with a short time and extend the activity than to have the students lose interest.

- **Keep the ideas flowing.** It is very common for students to run out of ideas quickly, often called *"hitting the wall."* To get things flowing again, you could have students read their list to help others start thinking of new ideas. Remind students that it is okay to "piggyback" on someone else's ideas, because sometimes a really unique idea can spark another good idea from someone else.

- **Accept all ideas.** Evaluating ideas should not happen during the brainstorm. If someone says *"That won't work"* or *"That's a stupid idea,"* then creativity is squelched and some students will stop sharing. If evaluation is a step you want to use, it comes later after all ideas have been freely given.

KWL CHART

K W L charts are a great grab-and-go strategy that accomplishes a lot in a short amount of time. This chart can be filled out individually, in small groups, or as a whole class.

To prepare a K W L chart, fold a piece of paper into thirds, similar to a letter. Title the first column "K," the second column "W," and the last column "L." Have students write the following in each column:

- **The K column:** What do I already **KNOW**? This step prompts students to tap into their prior knowledge.

- **The W column:** What do I **WANT** to know? Next, students ask themselves thoughtful questions about what new knowledge they are interested in learning.

- **The L column:** What have I **LEARNED**? Then, students check their own understanding after the lesson as they fill out the last column.

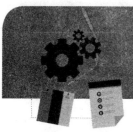

Graphic Organizers

Graphic organizers are handy tools for helping students visually organize and identify relationships between bits of information. Research has shown that using graphic organizers can really help students retain and make sense of material. Here are descriptions of two graphic organizers for you to try in your next class: Venn diagrams and concept maps.

VENN DIAGRAM

A Venn diagram is a terrific and artistic way to compare and contrast two or three ideas. To create a Venn diagram, the student or teacher will draw two circles partially overlapped.

For example:

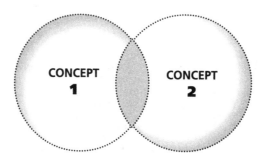

You can also compare and contrast three concepts by adding an additional circle.

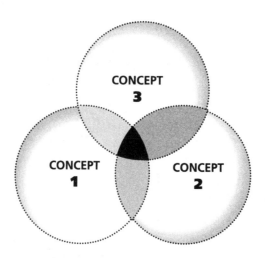

After drawing the diagram, the teacher or student should list a concept in each of the circles. List similarities in the areas where the circles overlap and differences where there is no overlap.

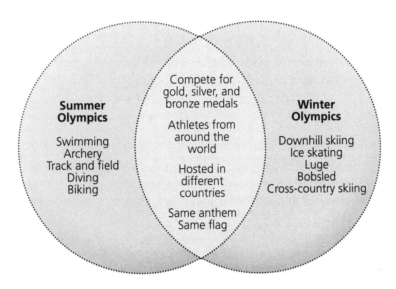

Summer Olympics

Swimming
Archery
Track and field
Diving
Biking

Compete for gold, silver, and bronze medals

Athletes from around the world

Hosted in different countries

Same anthem
Same flag

Winter Olympics

Downhill skiing
Ice skating
Luge
Bobsled
Cross-country skiing

Try whipping out a Venn diagram whenever the plans call for comparing topics, discussing differences, or referencing students' previous knowledge of two to three topics.

Note:

In addition to being classified as a graphic organizer, Venn diagrams can also be considered a lesson kickstarter organizer and a reviewing strategy.

For additional downloads, visit:
STEDI.org/ Handbook

CONCEPT MAPPING

Concept mapping, also known as webbing, is one of the most versatile and useful activities to pull out of your bag of tricks. This activity is perfect for introducing a new topic or checking to see what students have learned at the end of a lesson. It works great for an entire class, small groups, or individuals—plus, students in all grade levels will enjoy creating maps.

Start this activity by placing a word or idea in the middle of the board or on a piece of paper. Students then add key words branching out that describe what they know about or associate with the concept. Use lines to connect related ideas, adding new topics or words as you try to fill in all the empty space. If students are ready to take it to the next level, try having them incorporate examples and applications into their maps.

Using maps at the beginning of a lesson allows students share what they already know about the topic, so you don't have to waste time covering familiar material. As a follow-up activity, concept mapping can be fascinating as you and the students get to see how much their knowledge has expanded. It also works great as a review, because it helps students to take information they have read, heard, or observed and restate it using key words they understand.

Tip:

To review how to create a safe and risk-free learning environment, see page 12 in Chapter One.

The concept map is a great tool for students to use in completing writing assignments. For example, if students are required to write an essay, it may be difficult for students to dive right in. However, if students take a minute to organize their thoughts and prior knowledge into a concept map, a well thought out essay can be produced a lot easier.

Also, remember the key to successful concept mapping is to keep ideas free flowing. Encourage a supportive and risk-free environment, where no ideas get squashed, so everyone will feel safe to share.

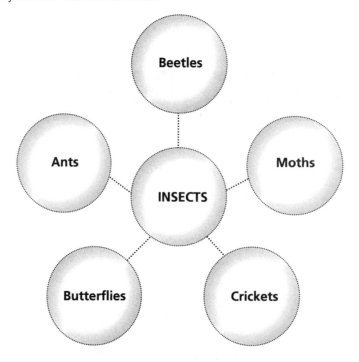

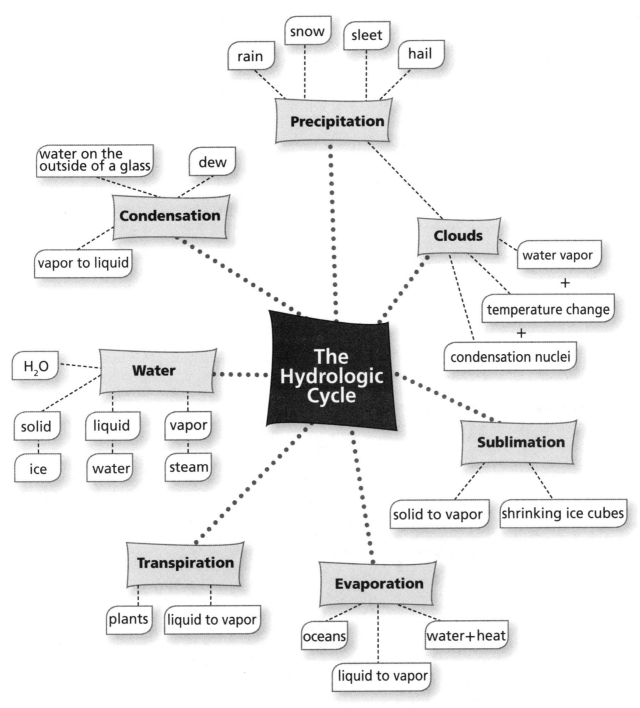

Note:

In addition to being classified as a graphic organizer, concept maps can also be considered a lesson kickstarter and a reviewing strategy.

Questioning
Strategies

Questioning Strategies

Occasionally, you might be asked to help students with a unit review or, better yet, you might even get a chance to directly teach something new. This can be one of your most rewarding experiences as a substitute teacher, because it's where the rubber meets the road and teaching happens! But sometimes class discussions can quickly run dry and become hard to manage. One of your best defenses against boredom and blank stares is asking excellent questions.

Why ask excellent questions?
- They help keep students on-task and focused.
- They help determine skill and knowledge levels.
- They promote higher-level thinking.
- They encourage broader student participation.

What makes questions excellent?
- They are logical and sequential.
- They fit the students abilities.
- They cause students to think, not just recite (see Bloom's Taxonomy on page 49).
- They encourage students to ask their own questions.

Avoid these common pitfalls so your excellent questions hit the mark.

Practice your patience!	Make it personal!
Sometimes teachers fall into this trap: they ask a question, then feel nervous during the few seconds of silence (when students are usually just thinking) and so they jump in and answer it themselves. This is one sure way to derail your discussion, because students quickly learn that you don't really expect them to answer the question. Sometimes you need to wait longer than you think is comfortable, so students actually feel stretched a bit and encouraged to get talking.	A question directed to the entire class sometimes seems like a question to no one. It's okay to direct your questions to specific students. You can even try creative ways of calling on different students like drawing names out of a jar, shuffling cards with students' names on them, or using a random name generator online.

Note that you should put the student's name back into the jar so they continue to stay engaged in the lesson. Assure students that it's okay to offer their best response, even if they don't know the answer, so everyone feels safe. |

THE ASK, PAUSE, CALL METHOD

Here's an easy method to remember:
ASK... a well thought-out question to the class.
PAUSE... long enough for students to think about a response.
CALL... on a specific student to respond to the question.

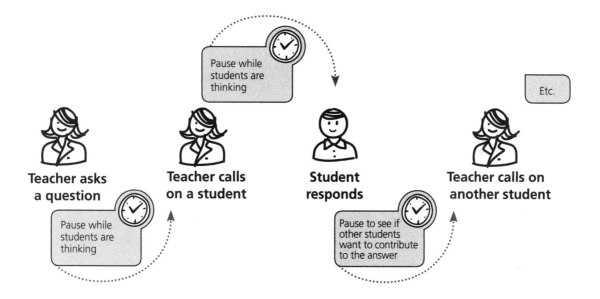

When asking questions, don't fear a little silence! Step up your bravery and try pausing after each step. For example, ask the question then pause for several seconds, which give students time to think about an answer (1st pause). Then, after you call on a specific student, pause again to give that student time to verbalize a response (2nd pause). You can even pause one more time after you ask for any other responses, which helps everyone think deeper about the question (3rd pause).

Note:

The Ask, Pause, Call Method can also be used as a reviewing strategy.

Pauses Cause Students to Think and Much More!

Did you know that most teachers only wait about one second when they're asking questions in class? A recent experiment showed that pausing for at least three seconds after you ask a question and then again after a student answers, can have some surprising positive consequences. It can even help to improve classroom discipline!

Learning to increase your wait time can be hard to do—but with practice, you can slow down the pace and have these great results* happen in your class:

- Students feel more confident in their answers with fewer *"I don't knows."*
- More students participate, not just the same small group.
- Students ask more of their own questions.
- Students elaborate more and give higher quality answers.
- Students listen to each other better.
- Teachers are more flexible when responding to a student's answer.
- Teachers are better at involving a variety of students, even lower performing students and students with special needs.

*Results shown in: "Wait Time: Slowing Down May Be A Way of Speeding Up!" by Mary Judd Rowe, Journal of Teacher Education. 1986.

What should I do when asking questions?
- Be positive and focus on what students DO know.
- Wait until the class is listening before asking a question.
- Ask questions in a clear and direct voice.
- Expect an answer.

What should I avoid when asking questions?
- Steer clear of rushing for an answer or answering it yourself.
- Try not to use discouraging language like, *"wrong," "not true," "incorrect,"* etc.
- Don't call on the same students over and over; give others a chance to share.
- Refrain from automatically repeating questions; instead teach them to listen the first time.

BLOOM'S TAXONOMY QUESTIONS TO PROMOTE HIGHER-LEVEL THINKING

Created by Dr. Benjamin Bloom

Bloom's Taxonomy is a famous system for helping students really *"bloom"* as thinkers and learners. As a teacher, you can learn how to ask excellent questions that range from simple knowledge to complex critical thinking. When a teacher asks the right type of questions, students progress from just recalling facts and figures, to being able to apply and evaluate new information in different situations.

Read through each level below, and notice how every time you move up a level, students are connecting more deeply with what they're learning. The important verbs that fit in each level are marked in bold.

Level 1: Knowledge-Level Questions

Knowledge-level questions ask students to **recognize, recall,** and **state** information like facts, terms, and basic concepts.

Sample Knowledge-Level Questions:
- **Name** the characters in the story.
- What is the capital of Wyoming?
- **Define** the word condensation.
- **List** the numbers between 23 and 45.

Level 2: Comprehension-Level Questions

Comprehension means students understand concepts at a basic level. They know the meaning of the information, but can't apply it to other situations yet.

Sample Comprehension-Level Questions:
- **List** three examples of plants.
- **Describe** the setting of the story.
- **Classify** the characters in the story as good guys or bad guys.
- **Compare** a cup of milk to a cup of water.

Level 3: Application-Level Questions

Application means students can use knowledge in a certain situation. They can apply rules, principles, and concepts in new and appropriate contexts.

Sample Application-Level Questions:
- Why is the sun important to life on Earth?
- **Using** what you have learned, how would you solve the following problem?
- How would schools be different without electricity?
- How much money would you have if you saved a dollar a day for seven years?

Level 4: Analysis-Level Questions

Analysis means students can **break down** a concept into its different parts.

Sample Analysis-Level Questions:
- Why did the boy in the story give away his gold coin?
- **Draw** the parts of a flower.
- **Explain** the differences between a raindrop and a snowflake.
- Which characters in the film were necessary for the plot?

Level 5: Synthesis-Level Questions

Synthesis means students can put together elements or parts to form a whole. They can **arrange** and **combine** pieces to form a pattern, structure, or idea that was not clear before.

Sample Synthesis-Level Questions:
- How could you change the characters' personalities to make them more likable?
- **Design** a new invention for…
- **Organize** the books you have read this year into three categories.
- **Prepare** a shopping list for Thanksgiving dinner.

Level 6: Evaluation-Level Questions

Evaluation requires the highest level of intellectual functioning. It means students not only understand the material but can also make a **judgment** about it.

Sample Evaluation-Level Questions:
- Should students be allowed to bring cell phones to school?
- Would you recommend this book/film to a friend? Why?
- How would the discovery of life on another planet affect the U.S. Space Program?
- Does the protection of an endangered species justify the loss of job opportunities?

For additional downloads, visit:
STEDI.org/ Handbook

Summary of Promoting Higher-Level Thinking

Knowledge
Level 1

Define, Draw, Repeat, Record, Label, Identify, Name, List

Name the author of the book.

Comprehension
Level 2

Classify, Compare, Contrast, Translate, Explain, Summarize, Give Examples

Compare the weather from yesterday with today.

Application
Level 3

Apply, Calculate, Compare, Demostrate, Illustrate, Practice, Solve, Use, Predict, Show

Complete the sentence using a vocabulary word from the lesson.

Analysis
Level 4

Analyze, Classify, Discuss, Divide, Explain, Infer, Inspect

Explain why it is important to have classroom rules.

Synthesis
Level 5

Arrange, Combine, Construct, Create, Design, Develop, Generalize, Organize, Plan, Categorize, Predict, Rearrange

Predict what would happen if a law was passed that made commercials on television illegal.

Evaluation
Level 6

Assess, Critique, Estimate, Evaluate, Judge, Rank, Rate, Recommend, Test, Value, Justify

What requirements for employing a new teacher would you recommend to the principal?

Note:

Using Bloom's Taxonomy to ask questions can also be used as a reviewing strategy.

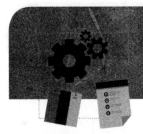

Group Work
Strategies

Group Work Strategies

Many lesson plans you encounter will lend themselves perfectly to group work. Working in a small group can help everyone stay active and has the added bonus of helping students practice real-life social skills as they cooperate with others. Here are some ideas for how to step out of the spotlight and put students in the driver's seat instead. As they interact with and teach each other, you'll be amazed at how they will step up.

COOPERATIVE LEARNING

In cooperative learning, your job shifts from presenter to organizer. Here are some basic tips for setting up a cooperative learning activity (developed by Dr. Carolyn Andrews-Beck). Note that putting students into groups comes after explaining what you'd like to see them accomplish. Once students know who else is going to be in their group, that is all they will focus on.

1. State the goal and instructions for the group work. Tell students that once they're in their group they should complete the following steps:
    A) Arrange themselves in a small compact circle so they can see everyone's face.
    B) Introduce themselves to their group.
    C) Complete these two statements as they begin:
        i.   "The job is..."
        ii. "We will know we have finished when..."
2. Set a time limit for the activity.
3. Question students about the expectations discussed so far. This should be done before assigning groups.
    A) "What should the group members do once they get into groups?"
    B) "How long do you have to complete the assignment?"
4. Divide the students into groups.
    A) Have students count off or form groups based on the seating arrangement.
    B) Do not let students self-select groups; it can lead to discipline problems.
    C) Keep the groups small (two to five per group).
5. Let the groups get to work!
6. Walk around and interact with each group to see how things are going and to help any groups that seem stuck.

Assigning Roles

To help the groups function smoothly, you can assign each member a specific role as they work. This method builds teamwork and makes sure that everyone is contributing.

Here are some common roles you can try using with groups:

- **Director, Captain, Leader, or Manager:** This person is the leader and is responsible for keeping the group members on task and working toward the goal.

- **Recorder:** This person records information for the group's activities, fills out worksheets, or prepares written material with help from the group.

- **Materials Manager:** This person picks up and returns equipment, materials, and supplies needed for the activity.

- **Procedure Director:** This person reads instructions, explains procedures, and makes sure the group is doing the activity correctly.

- **Cleanup Leader:** This person supervises the cleanup of the group's area at the end of the activity or project.

For additional downloads, visit:
STEDI.org/ Handbook

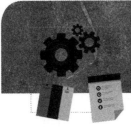

Jigsaw Learning Method

As you'll soon discover, one of the best ways to learn something is to teach it! Jigsaw Learning takes advantage of this fact by flipping things around and letting students have a chance to teach each other. It takes a bit of advanced preparation time, but can pack a real punch—especially when you need to cover a lot of material. You may want to avoid this activity with students younger than 4th grade. Older students will have an easier time understanding the process and responsibilities required of them.

Here's how Jigsaw Learning works with 25 students:

- Divide the learning material into five sections. (This could change based on the amount of material and the number of students in the class.)
- Use different colored dot stickers to represent each section and number each color 1-5.
- Distribute all the stickers, which will assign each student into two groups (one color and one number.)
- Arrange the classroom so students with the same colors sit together.
- Assign each color group a task to accomplish or a topic to study in a designated amount of time.
- After completing the assigned task, students rearrange into number groups where they teach each other the information they have "mastered" while in their color group.

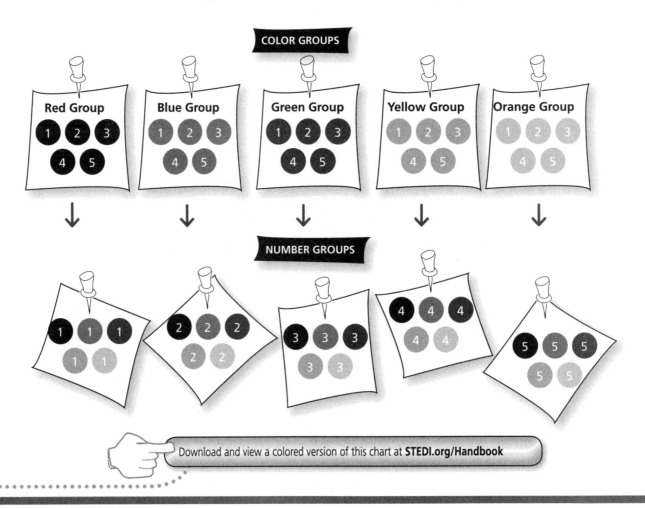

Download and view a colored version of this chart at **STEDI.org/Handbook**

Reviewing
Strategies

Reviewing Strategies

When the lesson plan calls for you to help students review a previous lesson or prepare for a test, don't succumb to something humdrum, get creative instead! Here are a few simple ideas that can help students recall and then retain information in fun ways.

SMART ART

Break out the crayons, butcher paper, watercolors, etc., and have students review the chapter using only pictures—no words. Students can create poster collages, artistic murals, or even 3-D models using basic classroom supplies. If you don't see what you need in your own classroom, stop by the office to see how you can get things from the school supply room. This activity is great for imaginative thinking because they get to use their right brain to review left-brained information.

Tell the class you will watch for contributions from each person, and be sure to keep groups small (two or three) so everyone gets to participate with their hands. Remind students that fun is the focus of this activity! They should avoid saying negative things about their ability to draw and just use the time to create and see the lesson material in a new way.

INVENT A GAME

Although games might seem like pure play, they are actually an excellent way to drill information. Divide students into groups of two or three, and have each group make a game to review the material you need to cover. Trivia games, memory games, and flashcard games...anything goes!

After giving students time to assemble their games and supplies, have each group pair up with another group and have a face-off. Try to allow for enough time to test both games, but feel free to expand or contract the activity to fill whatever time you need.

EXIT SLIPS

Try this method as an easy way to take inventory of what learning happened during the class period. Instead of a secret password, students need to present an exit slip to get by you and out the door. Near the end of class, hand each student a sticky note. You can direct them to write either the most important concept they reviewed that day, one thing they learned, or one question they still have about the information.

As the students leave the classroom, everyone sticks their note on the door. Afterward, you can take a minute to skim over the notes to see how things sank in during the day. You can also leave the stack of notes for the permanent teacher, which is a great way to give him a quick status of where the class left off.

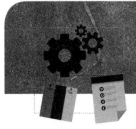

Teaching with Technology

As a substitute teacher, you'll often get the chance to use innovative classroom technology, such as an interactive whiteboard, video player, projector, or document camera. It's important for you to have a general knowledge of how to use each of these items before you walk into class. Here are some ways to up your skill level and become a more tech-savvy sub.

Search for Online Resources

Surveys have shown that substitute teachers who are handy with technology are offered more jobs. So take time to brush up by reviewing some resources online, like instructional videos on how to use document cameras or interactive whiteboards. Here are two excellent websites to start with:

- prometheanplanet.com
- exchange.smarttech.com

Ask for Help

If you find yourself faced with tricky technology, don't be afraid to ask the technical department, a neighboring teacher, or even students for a little help. Remember, arriving at least twenty minutes prior to the start of the day gives you time to investigate the classroom layout and technology you'll need.

Have a Back-Up Plan

As a substitute teacher, you might run into Murphy's Law when working with technology, meaning the one piece of equipment you need will be the one most likely to cause you grief! This is where having a well-stocked **SubPack** can be your best ally. You can quickly pull out something fun and engaging, and the class will never know it wasn't part of the original lesson plan.

Consider Your First Impression

For those who have been on a bad first date, we understand that first impressions stick! Although getting the interactive whiteboard or projector up and running is a top priority, consider the first impression students might have if they see you struggling with technology when they walk into class. It is important to have everything ready for the lesson, but it is even more important to be ready for the students. Greeting students at the door and helping them get settled will help you get off on the right foot. If you need more setup time, try giving students a longer starter activity to work on while you finish your preparations.

IMPORTANT NOTE ABOUT WHITEBOARDS:

Dry-erase boards and interactive whiteboards often look very similar. To avoid leaving your mark (permanently!) be sure to check before using any type of markers.

"Just Show the Video"

You will be sure to encounter this phrase many times during your career as a substitute teacher... *"Just show the video."* Although this may seem like you have the day off, sometimes it just leads to big problems in classroom management. The key to encouraging learning during a video is to involve students as active, rather than passive, viewers. Start by telling the students how they will be accountable for the information at the end. Here are some other tips that will also help you make the most of media.

Keep the Lights On

A darkened classroom is an open invitation for problems. Besides making everyone feel ready for a nap, some students will feel bolder about trying to get away with things they would never attempt in the light. A well-lit classroom is the appropriate status quo and makes it possible for students to take notes or complete assignments that go with the video.

Stand in the Back

You can also prevent problems, by staying "on the job" during the video. Sitting at the teacher's desk correcting papers or reading a book puts you at a disadvantage in heading off discipline problems. Consider standing at the back of the room, where it is easy to spot and correct trouble early.

Try making K-W-L Charts

Another easy idea is to assign individual K-W-L charts like the one found on page 41. Before the video, have students complete the first two columns about what they already know about the topic and what they might like to learn. Students can then complete the third column as they watch. You can even let students share their favorite "light bulb" learning moments after the video by making a combined list on the board.

Create Concept Maps

Concept maps also help students focus during a video, but have a little more pizzazz than just taking notes. Start by listing the main topic in the center of the page. As they watch, students can record key words and bits of information they are learning (see the example on page 44).

Think creatively about what students can do with their maps after the video. A few ideas are to have them expand their maps by sharing with a neighbor, turn them in for quick teacher feedback, or create a giant map on the board by allowing all students to come up front and write one thing from their own map.

Set up a Question Exchange

Here's a snappy way to help students stay active during the video and to interact with others after. While they watch, each student comes up with an allotted number of questions. Each question must fit these two criteria:

1. The answer must come from the video.
2. The student writing the question must know the answer.

Each student can then challenge others to an exchange after watching. Always be sure to plan enough time for the students to complete the question exchange. Otherwise, students may not take this activity seriously.

How Should I Do That?

Remember, when you're hired as a substitute teacher, you need to cover the material assigned by the permanent teacher. However, sometimes the lesson plan instructions are very general, leaving room for you to add a dash of originality in your presentation. Use this section as a review of the teaching strategies from this chapter, and consider how you could now enhance each lesson below. Remember there is always more than one way to present material, so challenge yourself to create a lesson using each of the categories.

LESSON PLAN ONE

You are assigned to teach a class of 32 seventh grade students. The plans say to have students read chapter 18 about volcanoes and answer the 20 questions at the end of the material. This activity should fill the entire 50-minute period. What strategies can you use to help students stay active and on task?

Lesson Kickstarter:	Graphic Organizer:	Group Work:	Reviewing Strategy:	Other Ideas:
Approx Time:	Approx Time:	Approx Time:	Approx Time:	Approx Time:

What activity will you use in case your plans end early?

....

....

....

For additional downloads, visit:
STEDI.org/ Handbook

LESSON PLAN TWO

Now you are in a high school honors English class. The teacher wants you to assign a persuasive essay about whether or not students should be allowed to have cell phones in class. The class period is 90-minutes long. What strategies would enhance this assignment and help you fill the time?

Lesson Kickstarter:	Graphic Organizer:	Group Work:	Reviewing Strategy:	Other Ideas:
Approx Time:	Approx Time:	Approx Time:	Approx Time:	Approx Time:

What activity will you use in case your plans end early?

....

....

LESSON PLAN THREE

You are to substitute teach in a fifth grade class with 27 students. The students have a test the next day about U.S. history. The teacher would like the students to review a packet of material about the Revolutionary War. You have 30 minutes until the recess bell rings. How would you respond?

Lesson Kickstarter:	Graphic Organizer:	Group Work:	Reviewing Strategy:	Other Ideas:
Approx Time:	Approx Time:	Approx Time:	Approx Time:	Approx Time:

What activity will you use in case your plans end early?

....

....

LESSON PLAN FOUR

Today you are substitute teaching in a second grade class. The teacher wants you to spend 20 minutes teaching the students about syllables. How are you going to fill the time?

Lesson Kickstarter:	Graphic Organizer:	Group Work:	Reviewing Strategy:	Other Ideas:
Approx Time:	Approx Time:	Approx Time:	Approx Time:	Approx Time:

What activity will you use in case your plans end early?

....

....

LESSON PLAN FIVE

You are in a ninth grade Spanish class of 40 students and the lesson plan says to show a video about the culture of Spain. The video is 25 minutes long, but you realize the class period is 45 minutes. How can you make the day a success?

Lesson Kickstarter:	Graphic Organizer:	Group Work:	Reviewing Strategy:	Other Ideas:
Approx Time:	Approx Time:	Approx Time:	Approx Time:	Approx Time:

What activity will you use in case your plans end early?

....

....

Gifted and Talented Students

RECOGNIZING GIFTED AND TALENTED STUDENTS

Gifted and talented students usually have above average ability, a high level of task commitment, and highly developed creativity. Many students will excel in one of these areas. Truly gifted students will excel in all three.

You may have a gifted student if he...
- has a vocabulary noticeably above his/her peers
- is a voracious reader—usually more advanced content
- has a well-developed sense of humor—gets jokes peers don't understand
- is intrinsically motivated—works hard with or without teacher approval
- has a personal standard of quality—independent of others' work
- thinks at a higher/independent level—often appears to *"day dream"*
- is able to go beyond basic lesson concepts—expand, elaborate, and synthesize

Often gifted and talented students seem to be round pegs in square holes. They do not necessarily fit the mold of an *"ideal student."* They may become bored with class or deeply involved with something unrelated to the lesson. Their friendships and alliances include a need for intellectual peers (often older students or adults) and chronological peers (kids their same age). Moreover, their attention span does not always coincide with the standard time allotments for classroom lessons and activities.

SOME DO'S AND DON'TS WHEN WORKING WITH GIFTED AND TALENTED STUDENTS

Do	Don't
• Enrichment and extension activities • Puzzles and games • Alternative projects (collages and posters are good) • Comparisons, similes, and analogies	• Make them do things they've already mastered • Give them busywork if/when they finish early • Force them to always work with slower students • Have them memorize, recite, and copy just to fill time

Some of the activities and lessons in Chapter Six have suggested accommodations listed. Use these accommodations for accelerated learners as appropriate. These accommodations are only suggestions. Think about other possibilities that could be used as you work with accelerated diverse learners.

Alternative Learning Styles

We are all different. We look different and we act differently. We also learn differently. Unfortunately, we tend to teach students as if they were all the same. We all know of people who can't bounce a ball, but can do math story problems in their head—or the person with two left feet who can sing like a bird. No one can do everything, but most of us do excel in one or more areas. It is in these areas that we learn best. By using a variety of teaching methods and activities that incorporate these abilities, we can increase students' ability to stay on-task, pay attention, and enjoy learning.

Here are some main categories of skills and abilities with a few examples of each:

Verbal Linguistic	Logical Mathematical	Visual Spatial	Body Kinesthetic
Reading	Calculation	Imagination	Dance
Writing	Formulas	Patterns/designs	Drama
Vocabulary	Codes	Sculpture/painting	Sports/games
Speech			
Interpersonal	**Intrapersonal**	**Musical**	
Group work	Self-reflection	Rhythms	
Empathy	Thinking strategies	Sounds/tones	
Cooperation	Reasoning skills	Singing/playing	

For additional downloads, visit: STEDI.org/Handbook

Using new ways to teach "old" materials might appeal to your students' particular abilities and interests. Here are some ideas:

Math	Language	History	Physical Education
• Compose a song to help remember a formula • "Illustrate" the problem on the board • Solve the problem as a group	• Act out the story • Write key words using a code • Listen with eyes closed	• Reenact a battle • Write a commercial for that time period • Do a mock interview of an historical person	• Research and play a historic game • Keep score using Roman numerals or fractions • Skip or hop instead of running

RUNNING OUT OF IDEAS?

Ask your students how they can turn a writing assignment into a math assignment, or how they can incorporate art into a soccer game. You'll be surprised at the results and your students will enjoy the challenge.

THE PROFESSIONAL
SUBSTITUTE TEACHER

*T*housands of surveys and interviews show permanent teachers, school administrators, and district personnel unanimously praise and value substitute teachers who are professional in dress, attitude, and presentation.

Being a polished and professional substitute teacher starts before your teaching day even begins and doesn't end when you leave the classroom. It involves many aspects of attitude and conduct that you should think about continuously as you develop as a substitute teacher. In this chapter, you'll learn how to present yourself professionally as we walk through five time frames:

- At Home

- Prior to Entering the Classroom

- In the Classroom Before School

- Throughout the Day

- At the End of the Day

Tip:

The top request of administrators and permanent teachers is that substitute teachers be prepared and professional.

1. At Home

There are a number of things you can do at home before you ever get that early morning call to substitute teach. Follow these tips to help you feel prepared for whatever the day may hold:

- **Prepare a set of note cards** or make a note on an electronic device for each school where you may be called to teach. On each note list the name of the school, principal, secretary, school phone numbers, start time, address, driving directions, and the approximate time it will take to get there. If there are certain classrooms where you prefer not to substitute teach, be sure you include those on the note cards.

- **Place a notebook and pencil by the phone you use to answer early morning calls.** You can even jot down any questions you want to ask when the call comes, such as, *"What is the name of the teacher and grade level where I will be substitute teaching?"*

- **Assemble a *SubPack*** filled with teaching supplies and activity ideas for the grade levels you teach. (For more information about a ***SubPack***, see page 76.)

- **Designate a section of your closet for substitute teaching clothes**. Assemble entire outfits, including shoes and socks, which are ironed and ready to go at a moment's notice. Be sure to choose comfortable shoes, since as an effective substitute teacher you will be on your feet all day. Have several different outfits ready so you are prepared to dress appropriately for different grade levels and subject assignments.

- **Answer the phone yourself** when the call comes. A groggy spouse or roommate does not always make a professional impression, and you will be wasting the caller's time while they are waiting for you to wake up and get to the phone.

APPROPRIATE ATTIRE GUIDELINES FOR MEN AND WOMEN

Research shows that teachers who dress professionally command more respect in the classroom than those who dress casually or inappropriately. Gain the respect you deserve by the way you dress.

As a general rule, jeans, T-shirts, sandals, and other casual clothing are not considered professional or appropriate for the classroom setting. You should always dress at least as professionally as your permanent teacher counterpart. Even if the school has casual days, be dressed a step above the permanent staff.

Women: Avoid uncomfortable shoes and clothing. Select outfits in which you can bend down, stoop over, and write on the board with ease.

Men: Consider wearing a shirt and tie. You can always remove the tie, undo the neck button, and roll up your sleeves if you find yourself "overdressed" for the assignment.

- **Make a plan.** After you hang up, take a look at your note card for the school, determine how long it will take you to get there, and plan the rest of the morning accordingly. Remember, you want to be at the school at least 20 minutes prior to either the beginning of class or when students arrive. Get ready and don't forget to grab your *SubPack* as you head out the door.

Tip:

FOR ACCEPTING LAST MINUTE CALLS

The hardest assignments for schools to fill are the early morning and last minute slots. Even though it isn't easy to accept last minute calls, it is a great method if you want to fill your schedule and get offered more jobs.

Try giving yourself a head start—pack your lunch, pick your clothes, and iron them the night before. The next morning, get up early and start getting ready at your normal time, while anticipating a call. If it doesn't come through, then you're still ready to start your day.

2. Prior to Entering the Classroom

Here are some suggestions for how to get your day off to a great start as soon as you enter the school building:

- **Arrive at the school enthusiastic about the day,** while serious about your role. If possible, arrive at least 20 minutes prior to the beginning of class. Report to the principal or office to let them know you have arrived, and ask these questions and any others you have:
  - Will I be responsible for playground, lunch, or other duties?
  - Do any of the students have medical problems I should be aware of?
  - If the need arises, how do I refer a student to the office?
  - How do I report students who are tardy or absent?
  - Do students need a pass to be in the halls during class time?

- **Obtain any keys** that might be necessary.

- **Find the locations** of restrooms, the staff room, the cafeteria, the auditorium, the media center, and the nearest drinking fountain before school begins.

- **Meet neighboring teachers.**

MEETING SCHOOL STAFF

Samuel Johnson, a famous English writer, once wrote, *"The happiest conversation is that of which nothing is distinctly remembered, but a general effect of pleasing impression."* Be sure to smile, and greet the school staff and other personnel you encounter by introducing yourself and thanking them for having you in the building for the day.

3. In the Classroom Before School

Try these quick ideas as you prepare for students to arrive:

- **Enter the classroom with confidence** and your *SubPack* at the ready. Put your name on the board and familiarize yourself with the room. Locate and review the classroom rules and evacuation map.

- **Read through the lesson plans** left by the permanent teacher and identify books, handouts, and papers that will be needed throughout the day.

- **Study the seating chart**. If you can't find a seating chart, get ready to make your own (see page 7).

- **Stand in the doorway and greet students** as they enter the classroom. Be professional, friendly, and enthusiastic about the day. This first impression will take you a long way.

MEETING STUDENTS

Research shows students "sum you up" in approximately two seconds, so this first impression is critical for setting the climate for the day. As you greet them with a smile, be sure to give a verbal reminder of what you are expecting them to do as they enter the classroom. This lets students know they are expected to get to work immediately and that it will not be a wasted day.

For additional downloads, visit:
STEDI.org/ Handbook

4. Throughout the Day

Keep these tips in mind as you interact with students:

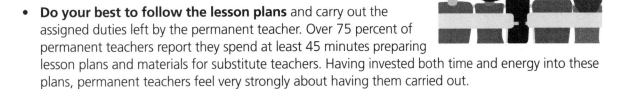

- **Do your best to follow the lesson plans** and carry out the assigned duties left by the permanent teacher. Over 75 percent of permanent teachers report they spend at least 45 minutes preparing lesson plans and materials for substitute teachers. Having invested both time and energy into these plans, permanent teachers feel very strongly about having them carried out.

- **Be ready for the unexpected.** You may enter a classroom where you are unable to locate the lesson plans or necessary materials. In this situation, report the problem to your grade level or departmental colleagues or to the office. It could simply be that plans have been emailed to someone who is not yet aware. Then, act quickly, calmly, and confidently to utilize materials and ideas in your SubPack, until someone brings you the plan. If one doesn't arrive, you will still have a productive day.

- **Work to bring out the best in each student.** Whatever situation or challenge you are faced with, always strive to be positive and respectful. Permanent teachers care about the students in their class. They want to see each student's strengths and weaknesses handled appropriately.

- **Build a positive relationship with students.** Permanent teachers urge substitute teachers to be aware of how small things, like using a respectful tone in your voice, giving praise, and having a positive attitude, can affect students. Students resent teachers who talk down to them, make promises or threats they don't intend to keep, and are not fair in administering rewards and consequences. Treating students as individuals is important. Don't blame the whole class or punish the group for the misdeeds of a few. (See Chapter One for suggestions on classroom management.)

- **Be an example.** When a substitute teacher uses good judgment, avoids criticism, and adapts to circumstances in a positive way, she becomes a professional role model for both the students and other teachers.

For additional downloads, visit: **STEDI.org/ Handbook**

5. At the End of the Day

Being professional is just as important at the end of the day as it is at the beginning. What you do just before the school day ends will be the impression students take home with them. How you leave the classroom will be the first impression the permanent teacher has of you when he returns.

BEFORE THE STUDENTS LEAVE

There are several things you should do during the last few minutes of class before the students leave:

- **Gather supplies and materials.** If the teacher has classroom sets (calculators, scissors, books, etc.), make sure they are all returned before the students leave the room. It is much easier to locate a missing calculator in a class of 30 than trying to find it somewhere in the whole school.

- **Challenge students to recall** and list on the board, projects and topics they have studied that day. (Now they will have a positive answer when parents ask what they did in school, instead of the traditional, *"Nothing, we had a substitute teacher."*)

- **Remind students of homework.** Writing homework assignments on the board throughout the day will help both you and the students remember.

- **Enlist the help of students.** Have students straighten and cleanup the area around their desks.

AFTER THE STUDENTS HAVE LEFT

After the students have gone, take a few minutes to complete your professional duties as a substitute teacher.

- **Fill out a Substitute Teacher Report** for the permanent teacher. Write a detailed summary of what was accomplished throughout the day, along with any problems that arose and notes about things that went well, or students that were particularly helpful. If, for any reason, you were unable to carry out the plans left by the permanent teacher, make sure you explain why you were unable to carry them out and what you did instead.

Visit **STEDI.org/Handbook** to print copies of a Substitute Teacher Report

- **Leave your contact information** and an invitation for the permanent teacher to get in touch with you if they have any questions or want to request you as their substitute teacher again in the future.

- **Leave the teacher's desk and assignments neatly organized**. Close windows, turn off lights and equipment, and double check to make sure the room is in good order before you lock the door and head for the office.

- **Return to the office** and turn in any keys, name badges, building folders, or any other materials given to you by the office staff. While you're there, express appreciation for the help you received, and check to see if you will be needed again the next day.

In Conclusion

Teachers have high expectations of others who come into their classroom and put a lot of trust in you as their substitute teacher. By following the ideas in this chapter, you can become a professional that meets and exceeds these expectations. Always remember you are a valued and important part of the educational system. Never diminish your role as a substitute teacher. Teachers appreciate having a person come into their classroom who is caring and capable. By being flexible, prepared, poised, and professional, you will greatly reduce the stress on the teacher, students, and yourself. The checklist on the following pages will help you stay on the right track throughout the day. Additional hints and suggestions are found at the end of Chapter One.

COMMUNICATING WITH THE PERMANENT TEACHER

Here are a few details to include in your Substitute Teacher Report

- **Leave positive feedback.** Let teachers know which students were cooperative and helpful. Try to avoid leaving negative feedback about particular students, which could make the permanent teacher feel that they need to intervene. Instead, leave detailed information as to what happened and how you handled it. This way the teacher is aware of the problem but can feel confident that you were able to handle the class.

- **Leave academic feedback.** Teachers often only receive feedback about student behavior. Be sure to let them know which students mastered the learning concepts, need a little review, and those who may need re-teaching.

- **Leave a personal note for the permanent teacher.** Let them know you enjoyed the class and would like to substitute teach for them again. Leave your name and number for them or even a business card you have created.

Note:

It is not professional to discuss a teacher's class with others, especially with people not associated with the school. You also should not discuss individual students or problems.

Professional Substitute Teacher Checklist

1. At Home

- ☐ Compile a set of note cards containing information about the schools where you may be assigned.
- ☐ Keep a notebook and pen by the phone to use to answer early morning phone calls.
- ☐ Assemble a **SubPack** and keep it well stocked and ready to go.
- ☐ Organize several appropriate substitute teacher outfits in a section of your closet.
- ☐ Leave early enough to arrive at school at least 20 minutes before the beginning of school.

2. Prior to Entering the Classroom

- ☐ Report to the principal or the office.
- ☐ Ask about student passes, playground rules, bus duty, lunch procedures, and other duties.
- ☐ Ask if there are any special duties associated with the permanent teacher's assignment.
- ☐ Find out how to refer a student to the office.
- ☐ Review the school's discipline policy.
- ☐ Ask if any children have medical problems.
- ☐ Obtain necessary keys.
- ☐ Ask how to report students who are tardy or absent.
- ☐ Find the locations of restrooms, the staff room, and other important places in the school.
- ☐ Introduce yourself to the teachers on both sides of your classroom.

3. In the Classroom Before School

- ☐ Enter the classroom with confidence and your **SubPack** ready to go.
- ☐ Put your name on the board.
- ☐ Review the classroom rules.
- ☐ Locate and review the school evacuation map and emergency procedures.
- ☐ Read through the lesson plans left by the permanent teacher.
- ☐ Locate books, papers, and materials that will be needed throughout the day.
- ☐ Study the seating chart. If you can't find one, be prepared to make your own.
- ☐ When the bell rings, stand at the doorway and greet students as they enter the classroom.
- ☐ Implement a starter activity.

4. Throughout the Day

☐ Greet students at the door and involve them in learning activities quickly.

☐ Carry out the lesson plans and assigned duties to the best of your ability.

☐ Improvise using the materials in your **SubPack** to fill extra time, enhance activities, or supplement sketchy lesson plans as needed.

☐ Be fair and carry out the rewards and consequences you establish.

☐ Be positive and respectful in your interactions with students and school personnel.

5. At the End of the Day

☐ Make sure all classroom sets are accounted for.

☐ Challenge students to recall projects and topics they have studied throughout the day.

☐ Remind students of homework.

☐ Have students straighten and clean the area around their desks.

☐ Complete a Substitute Teacher Report for the permanent teacher.

☐ Neatly organize papers turned in by students.

☐ Close windows, turn off lights and equipment, and make sure the room is in good order before you lock the door.

☐ Turn in keys and any money collected at the office.

☐ Thank individuals who provided assistance during the day.

☐ Check to see if you will be needed again the next day.

Tips for Getting More Substitute Teaching Jobs

The question asked again and again by substitute teachers is, *"How can I get more jobs?"* Although there is no single right answer to this question, in addition to the suggestions already given, below are other ideas of how to become a preferred substitute teacher in the schools where you work.

The pool for substitute teaching jobs can be competitive. But if you work on meeting each goal and put forth your very best effort every day, you will be sure to rise to the top!

Be available. The more frequently you say, *"Yes,"* when called for an assignment (especially those that are last minute) the higher the likelihood you will be called again.

Actively seek assignments. If your district uses an automated online system, be sure to search for assignments often. A great trick is to search early in the morning before the system begins calling. You will have your choice of assignments that were put in the system after the closing of the day. You may also want to network with other teachers in the faculty room, so you will be a familiar face.

Teach in special education classes. Assignments in this area can be especially difficult to find substitute teachers for, yet they are often the most fulfilling and enjoyable.

Advertise your degree. If you have a degree in a specialized area, be sure to introduce yourself to the building staff in that department.

Follow the lesson plans. The number one complaint of full-time staff is substitute teachers do not follow the plan left for them. Teachers spend a great amount of time and energy planning lessons, so they depend on you to keep the class on track.

Do whatever is asked of you with a smile.
If you are asked to cover an additional duty like recess, lunch, or bus duty, accept it cheerfully.

Ask if there is anything you can do to help out.
When you have unplanned time, be sure to offer to help colleagues. The art rooms and libraries are great places to offer help if your grade level/departmental colleagues have nothing for you to do.

Grade papers if the teacher requests you do so.
If you end up not having time to help with any grading you were asked to do, be sure to leave a note explaining how you used your prep time instead.

Work to improve your classroom management skills.
If the school/district offers training, be sure to attend.

Volunteer your time.
Sign up to help in a before or after school program if volunteers are needed. The permanent staff will always remember your effort and it will help you stand out.

Attend extra-curricular activities.
This helps you network with school staff and shows that you support the school.

Be selective.
If you have trouble in a specific classroom or curricular area, avoid it in the future. It is better to decline the assignments where you are not successful in order to get more jobs in the future!

Be reflective.
If you did not have the best day, take time to reflect on what went well and what you would do differently next time.

SubPack

Just like a prepared hiker or paramedic who carries a first-aid kit, a **SubPack** is like an emergency kit for the classroom and can help you be ready for anything. It should contain a variety of useful and necessary classroom supplies and materials. We'll show you how to pack a powerful kit that can be organized into these four categories: Personal and Professional Items, Classroom Supplies, Rewards and Motivators, and Activity Materials. You can tailor your **SubPack** to fit your personal teaching style and the grade levels you teach most often.

SUBPACK CONTAINER

When selecting a container for your **SubPack**, choose one that is easy to carry, large enough to hold all of your supplies, has a secure lid or closure device, and looks professional.

Supplies for Your SubPack

Classroom Supplies
- Rubber bands
- Markers and/or colored pencils
- Labeled ball-point pens (red, blue, black)
- Pencils and small pencil sharpener
- Transparent and masking tape
- Crayons
- Scissors
- Glue sticks
- Paper clips, staples, a small stapler
- Sticky notes (various sizes and colors)
- Ruler
- File folders
- Calculator
- Lined and blank paper
- Name badge materials (address labels or masking tape will work)

Rewards/Motivators
- Tickets*
- Certificates
- Stickers
- Mystery Box*
- Stamp and Ink Pad
- Privilege Cards (get a drink, first in line, etc.)

Personal/Professional
- Clipboard*

- Substitute teacher report
- District information (maps, addresses, phone numbers, policies, starting times, etc.)
- Coffee mug or water bottle
- Whistle (useful for P.E. and playground duty)
- Small package of tissues
- Snack (granola bar, pretzels, etc.)
- Small bag or coin purse for keys, drivers license, money (enough for lunch), and other essential items. Do not bring a purse or planner with a lot of money, checks, and credit cards (there may not be a secure place to keep it).
- Band-aids
- Small sewing kit with safety pins
- Disposable gloves and small plastic bags*

Activity Materials
- The *Substitute Teacher Handbook*
- Tangrams*
- Bookmarks
- "Prop" (puppet, stuffed animal, etc.)*
- Picture and activity books
- A number cube or dice for games
- Estimation jar*
- Newspaper*
- Timer or stopwatch

*Notes about SubPack Supplies

Here is some extra information about a few of the items previously listed:

- **Tickets:** Tickets are a great way to reward students for appropriate behavior. Students can use tickets to enter an end-of-the-day drawing or redeem them for special privileges and prizes.

- **Mystery Box:** Place a common item, such as a toothbrush or piece of chalk, in a small box. Allow students to lift, shake, smell, and otherwise observe the box throughout the day. At the end of the day, have students guess what is in the box and award a small prize to the student who identifies the contents correctly.

- **Clipboard:** Carrying a clipboard provides quick access to a seating chart, the roll, and any other records. It will also add to your credibility by helping you look like an authority figure.

- **Disposable Gloves & Plastic Bags:** Whenever you encounter blood or bodily fluids you should wear disposable gloves to help safeguard against many of today's medical concerns, but be sure to inquire in the building nurse's office, as there may be children with latex allergies. A plastic bag can be used in an emergency when you must dispose of items exposed to blood or bodily fluids.

- **Tangrams:** Tangrams are geometric shapes that can be used as filler activities and teach shapes and geometry. Tangrams available to print at **STEDI.org/Handbook.**

- **Props:** A puppet, magic trick, or even a set of juggling props can capture students' interest. Props provide great motivation to complete assignments in order to participate in, learn more about, or see additional prop-related activities.

- **Estimation Jar:** Setting out a fun estimation jar can be a great motivator for students. Let them earn guessing tickets as they show appropriate behavior and complete assignments efficiently.

- **Newspaper:** A newspaper can be used as the basis for a story starter, spelling review, current events discussion, and a host of other activities (see page 145).

Low Cost/No Cost Rewards and Motivators

In the ideal classroom, all students would be intrinsically motivated to behave appropriately and work hard on every assignment. However, this is not usually the case. Many substitute teachers experience success in motivating classes by providing rewards throughout the day. The following are ideas for low and no-cost rewards and motivators.

Certificates
Print blank certificates (found at **STEDI.org/Handbook**) to be filled out and given to exceptional students, groups, or the entire class at the end of the day or as prizes for classroom activities.

Pencils and Pens
Colorful variations of these school supply basics are well received at any grade level as contest prizes. They can often be purchased very inexpensively at discount and dollar stores.

Stickers
These can be given intermittently throughout the day to students who are on-task or placed on completed assignments to denote outstanding work.

Tickets
Throughout the day, students can be given tickets for being on-task, cooperating, and following directions. These good behavior tickets are then turned in for a drawing to win a special prize prior to going home.

Extra Recess Time
Being allowed five extra minutes of recess can provide tremendous motivation for many students. Be sure to check with the principal or neighboring teacher beforehand to make sure that this reward will not interfere with the schedule of anyone else in the school.

Privilege Cards
Individual students can be rewarded for good work or appropriate behavior with special privileges. You can make privilege cards that entitle students to things such as being first in the line, getting a drink, being the teacher's assistant for an activity, choosing the end of the day activity, etc. Laminate the cards and use a wipe-off marker—when the student redeems the privilege, collect the card and put it back in your *SubPack* for your next assignment.

Fun Activity
The promise of a fun activity later in the day can motivate students for hours. The activity might be a Five-Minute Filler or Short Activity from this book, or any other activity you think they would enjoy. Remember, being "fun" is usually anything that is different from the routine of an ordinary day.

Story Time
One successful substitute teacher uses the promise of a story at the end of the day to motivate classes. She brings to school an old pop-up book about a dinosaur. At the beginning of the day, the word "DINOSAUR" is written on the board. A letter is erased each time the students are off-task or behaving inappropriately. At the end of the day if there is any of the word "DINOSAUR" still left on the board, they get to hear the story. Second-hand book stores are a good place to look for inexpensive books that your students will not have seen before.*

*Submitted by Marilyn Machosky of Sylvania, Ohio

Estimation Jar

Fill a jar with pennies, marbles, beans, or rubber bands. Recognize students who are on-task, setting a good example, or working hard, by giving them a slip of paper to write their name and guess the number of items in the jar. The more times they are recognized for good behavior throughout the day the more chances they have to "guess." At the end of the day, reveal the total number of items in the jar and award a prize to the student whose guess was the closest.

Talk Time

Middle school students really like moving to another seat and being allowed to sit and talk with friends during the last five minutes of class. To ensure an orderly classroom, you may need to insist that students select their new seat and then not get up until class is over. Elementary students also enjoy this activity while waiting to go to lunch or at the end of the day.

NOTES FOR THE TEACHER

Establish rewards and motivators not as "bribes to be good," but as "goals" that students can work toward and achieve through good behavior and diligent effort.

For additional downloads, visit:
STEDI.org/ Handbook

Getting a Permanent Teaching Job

Like many substitute teachers, you might be working toward getting a permanent teaching assignment and a classroom of your own. Here are a few proven suggestions for you to try as you pursue your goal:

Be Proactive.
Let your intentions be known! Meet with principals and district personnel early in the year to let them know you are excited about working in the district and hope, at some point, to be offered a permanent teaching position.

Be Available.
Districts are looking for people who are dependable. Once you have signed up to substitute teach, try to be available to teach whenever you are needed. Your willingness to fill in at the *"last minute"* will make a lasting, favorable impression on those making personnel decisions later in the year.

Be Professional.
You should consider yourself a real teacher in the school district. That means acting, dressing, and speaking appropriately at all times. If the school knows you want to be hired for a permanent job, remember that they will be watching everything you do throughout the year.

Be Willing to Go the Extra Mile.
Arrive early and stay late. You can also volunteer to help with after school activities.

Be Positive.
Just like your mother always told you, *"If you can't say something nice, don't say anything at all."* Anything negative you say about a school, principal, or teacher will eventually come back to haunt you. Stay positive and compliment those around you whenever possible.

Be Confident.
Walk tall—teach with confidence, but don't be overbearing.

Be Open to Feedback.
Don't assume one bad experience or evaluation will take you out of the running. Learn from the experience and ask for advice from other teachers or principals. You can even ask for positive evaluation forms or letters of support/recognition to be filed at the district office.

Be Willing to Grow.
Attend workshops sponsored by the district. Some districts even invite substitute teachers to attend professional development workshops scheduled for permanent teachers. You may also consider subscribing to current education journals or magazines. This shows that you are serious about a career in education and want to stay current with what is happening in the profession. Check with library personnel for subscription information.

Be "In the Know."
One of the most commonly used phrases in prospective teacher interviews is, *"Are you familiar with…"* By illustrating your knowledge of special programs, textbooks, or the mission statement of a district, you show you are interested and up-to-date with what is going on in the district. Applicants who are familiar with district programs and practices have a better chance at getting a job.

CHAPTER 4

SPECIAL EDUCATION

$\mathcal{E}$ach day in the United States millions of children go off to school, all with different strengths and weaknesses, abilities and inabilities. Over five million of these children have been identified as having a specific disability such as a learning disability, cognitive impairment, autism, or emotional disturbance that necessitates some type of special instruction. Teachers who work with these unique students every day need to be able to count on caring and capable substitute teachers for when they are away.

As a substitute teacher, you will have the opportunity to teach in a variety of special education settings. This chapter outlines how special education service locations are set up, the skills you need to enter these locations with confidence, and a brief description of the various disabilities you may encounter with guidelines to help you make the most of your assignment.

Why Substitute Teach in Special Education?

Every child brings unique abilities and possibilities into the school setting. Uniqueness and diversity are the capstones that make special education classrooms so dynamic. Whether or not you have worked with children with disabilities previously, your presence in special education classrooms is needed and worthwhile. The experiences give you the opportunity to do great work for great people.

There are numerous rewards for substitute teaching in special education classes. Perhaps the most valuable is the feeling that you have helped to improve the lives of children with disabilities. Another benefit is that in dedicated special education classes, you rarely work alone because many people work together to make the class successful.

Substitute teachers have the opportunity to teach in a variety of special education settings. This chapter outlines how special education service locations are set up, the skills you need to enter these locations with confidence and make your day a great success, and a brief description of various disabilities you may encounter with guidelines to help you make the most of your assignment.

THE SPECIAL EDUCATION SERVICE LOCATION

Special education usually encompasses an integrated set of several individualized services, not necessarily a location. However, to familiarize you with what special education may look like, here are some possibilities:

- A general education classroom with some students with special needs who spend all or part of their day in the classroom with or without support from paraprofessionals
- A resource room where students are pulled from their classrooms for small periods of the day
- The special education teacher spending time in multiple general education classrooms, co-teaching with the general education teacher with mixed groups of students
- A self-contained classroom with students with similar disabilities (e.g., a classroom with only students with autism)

The diversity may seem challenging, but can be very fun if you are up for adapting to an array of experiences throughout your day and from assignment to assignment.

Special Education Skills

No matter what your specific special education classroom may look like, there are several skills that you can practice that will make your day go smoothly. Also, by remembering the principles of behavior outlined in Chapter One and practicing the teaching strategies in Chapter Two, you will be well-prepared for any classroom. In this section, a number of skills are discussed that are particularly important in a special education setting, including:

- Having an Attitude of Respect
- Working with Paraprofessionals
- Being Familiar with Special Education Terms and Laws
- Maintaining Instructional Consistency
- Adapting Lessons and Activities
- Knowing Students and Meeting All Their Needs

HAVING AN ATTITUDE OF RESPECT

When you interact with students with disabilities or special needs, be respectful of them as individuals and treat them with dignity. The way you talk about them can reveal your attitude toward them. Use language that refers to the student as a person with a disability, not a disabled person. Do not use demeaning words like *"crippled," "handicapped,"* or *"retarded."*

The way you talk to them can also reveal your attitude toward them. Talk directly to the student, not to the paraprofessional or other helper that may be with them. Be welcoming and caring, but don't baby them or feel sorry for them. As with all students, you want to be firm and fair.

Recognize that students with disabilities have individual differences—both from their nondisabled peers and also from other students that have the same or similar disability. But also remember that students with disabilities or special needs, like all students, have a lot in common with their peers.

Confidentiality is particularly important when working in a special education setting. Refrain from talking about students to anyone who does not work with them. Any private details about a student's disability or program that you learn or hear about should remain private. A good rule of thumb to follow is the phrase, "Need-to-Know Basis." Which means, does the person you are about to share the information with need to know it in order to help the student? If not, don't say anything. For example, a spouse doesn't need to know who is in a resource class. Information you share on a need-to-know basis should only go to school district personnel and parents/guardians—assume that others do not need to know.

WORKING WITH PARAPROFESSIONALS

One of the greatest benefits of working in a special education classroom is the amount of support generally available from experienced paraprofessionals. You can use their individual expertise about classroom procedures and specific students to make your day successful. It is important, however, that

you remember that you are substituting for the teacher, not the paraprofessional. Be willing to delegate when appropriate. Here are some other tips:

- Define your working relationship early. You are the teacher, which means you are responsible for ensuring that the lesson plans are carried out.
- Ask questions to clarify your responsibilities. After reading the lesson plans, ask any questions you have about the classroom routines, students, or specific responsibilities with the paraprofessional. Define what you and the paraprofessional(s) will do in case of emergency. Do not think that asking questions or asking for help makes you appear less capable.
- Let the paraprofessional do his/her job. The classroom paraprofessional may be willing and able to assume some degree of authority for conducting classroom activities. Some students may work better with a familiar face. Discuss roles and responsibilities with the paraprofessional before issues develop.
- Respect the paraprofessional's level of knowledge and expertise. Be teachable. The paraprofessional knows the classroom and the students. You can value their experience without diminishing your own.

BEING FAMILIAR WITH SPECIAL EDUCATION TERMS AND LAWS

As a substitute teacher, you need to have a basic understanding of terms and acronyms used in special education settings. The following are some key terms and a brief synopsis of special education laws that you should be familiar with.

KEY TERMS

Assistive Technology: The use of devices that increase the ability of students to get along in society or that improve their quality of life (wheelchairs, computers, hearing aids, etc.).

IEP Team: A group of educational and related service personnel who develop, carry out, and evaluate the individual education plan, or IEP.

Individualized Education Plan (IEP): An individualized, written program that is developed and carried out by the members of the IEP team.

Behavior Intervention Plan (BIP): A plan written by the IEP team for an individual student that specifically outlines what procedures and practices will be used to reinforce positive behaviors and decrease undesirable behaviors.

Curriculum-Based Assessment (CBA): The practice of obtaining direct and frequent measures of student performance based on a series of objectives from a classroom curriculum.

Inclusion: Involving students with disabilities as active participants in general education classroom activities.

Least Restrictive Environment: A location in which students have a maximum opportunity to interact with students who do not have disabilities.

FIVE EFFECTIVE, OR ATTITUDINAL, BENEFITS OF INCLUSION ARE:

1. The students without disabilities learn to be more responsive to others.
2. New and valued relationships develop.
3. Students without disabilities learn something about their own lives and situations.
4. Students learn about values and principles.
5. Students gain an appreciation of diversity in general.

PUBLIC LAW 94-142 (INDIVIDUALS WITH DISABILITIES EDUCATION ACT)

Passed in 1975 and updated most recently in May 2004, The Education for All Handicapped Children Act has been amended and is now called IDEA or the Individuals with Disabilities Education Act. It entitles all students with disabilities between the ages of 3 and 21 to free, appropriate public education. Presently, the terms disability and disabled are used in place of handicap and handicapped.

The law defines individuals with disabilities to include those who are cognitively disabled, hard of hearing, deaf, speech impaired, seriously emotionally disturbed, or orthopedically impaired; have multiple disabilities; or have other health impairments or learning disabilities and therefore need special educational services.

IDEA also provides ALL students with disabilities with the right to be served in the least restrictive environment—this means that they must be educated and treated in a manner similar to their nondisabled peers. This usually consists of placing children with disabilities in the regular classroom.

WHO DECIDES HOW CHILDREN WITH DISABILITIES WILL BE EDUCATED?

IDEA requires that a team consisting of the student, his/her parent(s), teachers, principal, and other professionals develop an individual education plan (IEP) detailing the goals and objectives of the educational services to be provided. The IEP lists all special and regular activities that the student will participate in.

SECTION 504

This section of the Rehabilitation Act of 1973 prohibits discrimination against people based on their disability. Students may not be left out of a public school activity only because of a disability. The major difference between Section 504 and IDEA is that the definition of a "disability" is broader under Section 504. In addition to the categories of disability mentioned above, it covers students with AIDS, tuberculosis, hepatitis, allergies, asthma, diabetes, heart disease, and many others that may not be covered by IDEA.

MAINTAINING INSTRUCTIONAL CONSISTENCY

When working in a special education setting, you will often work with students who need <u>structure and consistency</u>. Therefore, it is extremely important that you follow the lesson plans left by the permanent teacher and follow the same classroom procedures. Some undesirable behaviors from students can be avoided by maintaining their structured routines. Carefully note the daily schedules for each student. They often have related service personnel (language or hearing specialists, occupational therapists, and physical therapists) come into the classroom. At other times they may leave the classroom to attend classes in other school locations.

IDEAS FOR ADAPTING LESSONS/ASSIGNMENTS

- Be patient and smile.
- Increase confidence, compassion, and cooperation by reinforcing success.
- Reduce the difficulty of activities/assignments (for students with barriers due to physical or emotional disabilities).
- Structure tasks so that the student does an easier task that s/he is more successful at after a difficult task .
- Provide breaks between tasks or assignments.
- Break a large task into several smaller ones.
- Repeat, rephrase, and redirect instructions and questions.
- Use a lot of examples.
- Model, review, practice, practice, practice. For example, *"I do one and you do one,"* or *"I do part and you do part."*
- Provide patterns or steps to follow.
- Read aloud.
- Move the student's desk for better hearing, seeing, and monitoring.
- Speak more slowly.
- Speak louder.

 IDEAS FOR ADAPTING GAMES/ACTIVITIES

- Reduce the size of the playing area.
- Adjust the boundaries, or change the number of players. For example, lower the net or basket.
- Use walls, fences, or designated "helpers" to aid in keeping the ball in-bounds.
- Find bigger/lighter equipment.
- Incorporate plastic bats, rubber racquets, jumbo gloves, enlarged hoops, expanded goals, etc.

Use the suggestions above and the adaptations included with the activities in Chapter Six and online to determine what accommodations may be appropriate for the students you work with.

KNOWING STUDENTS AND MEETING ALL THEIR NEEDS

Meeting the needs of individual students requires sensitivity to their behaviors and developing a keen ability to communicate with each student. Some students have specific needs involving medical issues, transportation, materials, and strategies for instruction and behavior. Be as attentive as possible to the students and keep the following guidelines in mind:

- The permanent teacher knows the students, what is required by their IEP (individualized education plan), and has drawn up lesson plans to meet those needs.
- You may need to stay in close proximity to offer assistance. A gentle reminder will often be enough to help the students stay focused.
- Use the student's name first to get his/her attention (e.g., *"Phoebe, please place the paper in the trash."* Avoid *"Place the paper in the trash, Phoebe."*).
- You may need to repeat yourself more often than usual. Be patient. Check for student understanding (e.g., *"Phoebe, please tell me what I asked you to do."*).
- Be flexible. Schedules can change and students may be transitioning in and out of the general education setting throughout the day.
- Be aware that some students may have experienced years of failure. Help them find success by recognizing and praising small successes.
- In class discussions, if a student responds with an incorrect answer, provide clues or a follow-up question to help him/her think of the correct answer.
- Look for ways to praise students for their thinking, behavior, and correct answers.
- Deal with a student individually if problems arise. Do not single him/her out in front of the class.
- Present short and varied instructional tasks planned with the students' success in mind.
- Allow students to use learning aids to assist them with their work as directed by the instructions left by the permanent teacher.
- Check with a paraprofessional, the principal, or another teacher before using any specialized teaching equipment or machines.
- Do not hesitate to ask for assistance from the principal or another teacher if you have concerns or questions during the day.

The following section offers strategies for working with students who have a particular need. However, you can feel confident that the strategies you have already learned in Chapter One: Classroom Management and Chapter Two: Teaching Strategies will still be effective for all students, including those with special needs.

CHARACTERISTICS OF DISABILITIES AND APPROPRIATE STRATEGIES FOR WORKING WITH THEM

You may encounter a variety of disabilities in your special education assignments. Federal legislation has identified specific disability categories that are covered under the Individuals with Disabilities Education Act (IDEA). Several types of disabilities (autism, blindness, deafness, emotional disorders, learning disabilities, cognitive impairment, multiple disabilities, orthopedic impairment, other health impairments, speech/language impairments, and traumatic brain injury) are described below. Keep in mind the following suggestions when working with students facing these challenges.*

* Adapted from Enhancing Skills of Paraeducators: A Video-Assisted Training Program, Second Edition, Robert L. Morgan et al, 2001. ISBN 1-931975-19-1, Technology, Research, and Innovation in Special Education (TRI-SPED), Utah State University.

Autism

Autism is a variable developmental disorder that is characterized by impairment of the ability to form normal social relationships and by impairment of the ability to communicate with others. Autism can affect language, measured intelligence, rate of development, and responses to people, events, and objects. Autism affects each person differently and its characteristics can fall anywhere on a spectrum that ranges from mild to severe. Students with autism may not communicate or socialize in typical ways. They may also preoccupy themselves with objects or items that seem unimportant. You might see other behaviors such as body rocking, head banging, unusual and repetitive hand movements, uncommon posturing, or repeated speech.

Students with autism need explicit assistance to identify cues for social occasions and respond in ways considered appropriate by others. When interacting with students with autism, use the communication system they use. Many students with autism require a very structured classroom, clear expectations, fast-paced instruction, and positive consequences for acceptable behavior. Keep classroom activities as regular and predictable as possible.

Blindness or Low Vision

Students are legally blind if they can see (with glasses) at 20 feet what other people see at 200 feet. Because of their severely impaired or nonexistent vision, they need assistance in understanding their place in space and may read using the Braille language. Students with low vision may use computers or books with large print.

When working with students who are blind, be sure to keep the classroom environment and layout consistent. Find out what assistive devices the student uses and allow those devices to be readily available. Ask students if you may assist them in moving from one place to the next.

Deaf or Hearing Impaired

Deafness is severe hearing loss to a degree that a student can't hear spoken language even with hearing aids. A hearing impairment is less severe but still affects classroom performance. Some deaf students or students with hearing impairments may have delays in their speech or language development and may use alternate forms of communication (sign language, communication boards, or computers).

Speak clearly with your face and lips in full view of the student. Do not talk loudly unless the student asks you to. Use the form of communication that the student uses.

Emotional Disorders

Students with an emotional disorder may display a range of behaviors different from those expected in a classroom. The behaviors may include aggression, violence, verbal threats, destruction of property, seeking attention inappropriately, tantrums, hyperactivity, compulsiveness, impulsiveness, irritability, or withdrawal. Students with an emotional disorder may seem to be unable to control their behavior. They may appear to have poor memory, a short attention span, or a poor image of themselves.

Give students with emotional disorders genuine praise for their success. Point out the student's successes so she can build her self-esteem. Make expectations small and achievable. Maintain trust by making eye contact, talking in a straightforward way, and listening carefully.

Learning Disabilities

Generally, students with learning disabilities have challenges affecting information processing (input and output of language), perception (distinguishing letters, numbers, and symbols), memory (auditory or visual), or attention (distractibility). These students may have problems in reading, writing, spelling, math, listening, or speaking. They do not learn at expected rates and may become frustrated, angry, or withdrawn.

Try to understand the student's frustration, but don't accept *"I don't know"* as an answer. Allow more time to complete the assignment. You may even have the student speak the answers rather than just having him write the answers.

Cognitive Impairment

Sometimes cognitive impairment is called intellectual disability. Intellectual characteristics and adaptive behavior among students with cognitive impairment are significantly below average. Students are classified with cognitive impairment before age 18 based on their low IQ score and limited adaptive behaviors (personal and social standards).

Students with cognitive impairment learn more gradually than their peers and consequently their skills are often delayed in comparison to their peers without disabilities. If students have mild limitations, they need special instruction but they are still able to communicate, respond to instructions, and care for themselves. Students with severe impairment need intensive instruction, have limited communication skills, and require training to care for themselves.

> Effective interaction with students with cognitive impairment will depend on the specific student. Use clear and simple language and check for understanding. Get the student's attention (say name and make eye contact) before giving instructions. Break tasks into small parts.
>
> Recognize students when they are successful and be specific in your praise. Students will often imitate what they hear and see, so always model appropriate social behaviors.

Multiple Disabilities

The multiple disabilities category is for students with two or more disabilities, like cognitive impairment and cerebral palsy, or blindness and deafness. Students with multiple disabilities need highly specialized instruction dependent on their specific needs.

> Use the appropriate descriptions and helpful tips included in the other categories as you interact with students with multiple disabilities.

For additional downloads, visit: **STEDI.org/ Handbook**

Orthopedic Impairments

Physical and neurological disabilities fall into this category. These include cerebral palsy, spina bifida, and muscular dystrophy. Students may use assistive technology devices for mobility, communication, or independence. Characteristics of these students vary based on the type and severity of the impairment.

Appropriate interaction depends on the specific characteristics of the student. Some students may require physical lifting or transferring. Be sure that the paraprofessionals or other staff in the classroom handle these procedures. They have been trained in correct body positioning so they do not injure the student or themselves.

- Students with cerebral palsy experience physical and neurological problems because of damage to the nervous system that occurred before, during, or immediately after birth. The student's muscles may be rigid and contracted. Coordination, mobility, balance, and communication may be affected.
- Students with spina bifida experience a birth defect of damage to the spinal cord. Students may experience motor impairment, muscle weakness, or paralysis.
- Muscular dystrophy is the progressive deterioration of muscles connected to the skeleton so students have limited muscle movement and mobility.

Other Health Impairments

These impairments are those not covered in the other categories. Students with disabilities are classified here if they experience attention-deficit problems, epilepsy, heart conditions, tuberculosis, rheumatic fever, nephritis, asthma, sickle cell anemia, hemophilia, lead poisoning, leukemia, arthritis, or diabetes.

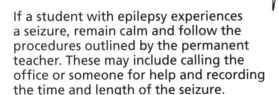

If a student with epilepsy experiences a seizure, remain calm and follow the procedures outlined by the permanent teacher. These may include calling the office or someone for help and recording the time and length of the seizure.

When working with students with attention-deficit problems, keep in mind that they have difficulty concentrating on tasks in the classroom and may appear impulsive or out of control. They are easily distracted. It is helpful if you have the student sit where they will not be disturbed by people passing by their desk. Keep instructional materials and manipulatives (or educational toys) out of the student's reach until it is time to use them. Describe expectations positively instead of stating what they should not do. Let the students learn by doing hands-on activities. Keep instruction fast-paced if the student appears bored or slow it down if s/he appears hyperactive.

Speech or Language Impairments

Speech impairments include articulation problems (abnormal production of sounds), stuttering (speech fluency), and voice problems (too loud, soft, or hoarse). Language impairments can include receptive (understanding spoken or written communication) or expressive (speaking clearly) problems. Often, these impairments affect academic skills.

Be supportive and reassuring—students are sometimes self-conscious of their disorder and may give up easily. Listen carefully and patiently and use clear and simple instructions.

Traumatic Brain Injury

Students in this category have experienced severe head injuries. Depending on the part of the brain that was injured and the severity of the damage, the student's speech, language, memory, motor function, intelligence, and behavior may be affected.

Use understanding, patience, and encouragement as the student works toward recovering abilities and skills.

In Conclusion

Special education teachers find their jobs very enjoyable and rewarding. As you spend time working with students with special needs, you will also find satisfaction at the end of the day.

Remember, all of the skills presented in this handbook can and should be used in special education settings. The skills presented in Chapter One: Classroom Management are based on 35 years of research and trials conducted by a special education professor. They have been used in countless regular and special needs classrooms worldwide, and combined with the additional skills presented in this chapter, you will be equipped to have an effective and rewarding substitute teaching experience in any classroom.

OTHER THINGS
YOU SHOULD KNOW

*C*hapter Five is a compilation of important information that you should know as a substitute teacher. While its contents are not comprehensive, it covers the basics for the following critical aspects of teaching:

- Safe Schools Policy
- First Aid and Safety
- Emergency and Evacuation Procedures
- Legal Aspects of the Job
- Child Abuse Reporting
- Sexual Harassment
- Being Sensitive to Diversity
- Bullying
- Out-of-Classroom Activities

The information presented here should be used as a review of general guidelines. Be sure to find out about policies, procedures, and state laws related to your specific district and school. Don't be afraid to ask fellow teachers, school administrators, or district personnel questions you might have about these or other topics.

Safe Schools Policy

Most school districts have established a Safe Schools Policy to foster a safe environment for students, staff, community, neighbors, and visitors where learning takes place without unnecessary disruptions.

Although each district has its own version/edition of a Safe Schools Policy, some general guidelines usually apply. Generally school administrators have a school-wide behavior management program in place, which could include:

- A variety of positive reinforcements
- A variety of consequences for inappropriate behavior
- A plan for serious misbehavior
- High visibility of teachers, staff, and administration
- Early intervention programs
- Special training programs
- Parent involvement
- Written policies on expulsion and suspension
- Accommodations for students with special needs

Students also have requirements and restrictions including:

- Knowing and complying with the school's rules of conduct
- Complying with all federal, state, and local laws
- Showing respect for other people
- Obeying people in authority at the school

Note:

Your district's Safe Schools Policy may be included with your substitute teaching orientation material. If not, be sure to request a copy from your district office and review it thoroughly.

First Aid and Safety

Common sense is the best resource when handling most classroom and playground accidents. Students who are injured should be sent to the office where a school nurse or secretary can administer first aid. However, don't fall into the trap of allowing students to go to the office for band-aids or ice for fake injuries. In the event of a severe injury, do not move the student. Instead, remain with the student, send another student or teacher for help, and try to keep the other students calm.

Never give medication to a student, not even aspirin. If a student requires medication, it should be administered through the school nurse, secretary, or other designated medical personnel.

You should also be prepared to handle situations involving blood and other bodily fluids. Listed below are the OSHA Universal Precautions for dealing with these situations. Contact the school district to find out the specific district policies and procedures that should be followed.

OSHA Universal Precautions for Handling Exposure to Blood/Bodily Fluids

- All blood/bodily fluids should be considered infectious regardless of the perceived status of the individual.
- Avoid contact with blood/bodily fluids if possible. Immediately notify the school nurse, administrator, or her designated first aid person.
- Allow the injured individual to clean the injury if possible.
- If it is not possible for the individual to clean the injury, disposable gloves should be worn. Gloves are to be discarded in a designated lined bag or container.
- Clothing that has been exposed should be placed in a plastic bag and sent home with the individual.
- Upon removal of gloves, hands should be washed thoroughly with warm water and soap.
- Surfaces contaminated with blood/bodily fluids should be cleaned thoroughly with disinfectant. The cleaning should be completed by the custodian, administrator, or designated individual responsible for cleanup.

As a general rule, do not touch a student who is bleeding even if you use gloves. If a student has a bloody nose or cut knee, hand him the box of tissues or paper towel, instruct him to hold it on his wound, and then send him to the office or school nurse for further care. Students who are bleeding should not be allowed to participate in class activities until the bleeding has stopped and the wound has been cleaned and completely covered.

Note:

- *Handle accidents with common sense.*
- *Only the school nurse or other designated personnel should administer first aid, including dispensing medication.*
- *Do not move a severely injured student.*
- *Learn and follow school district policy for handling situations involving blood/bodily fluids.*
- *Always remain with the class and send a student or another teacher to get help when needed.*

ADVICE FROM SCHOOL NURSES
for Substitute Teachers*

▷ Do not dispense medication (prescription or over-the-counter) to any students. Send them to the office or school clinic where they have a record of the written permission to give the student the medication, the prescribed amount, and a system for recording the times and dosage administered.

▷ Refer all students with injuries (even minor ones) to the office so the normal school procedures can be followed. In an emergency, you may need to ask another student to escort the injured student to the office or solicit help.

▷ Carry a pair of disposable gloves that are waterproof and made of either latex or vinyl, for use in the event of an emergency that requires you to come in direct contact with a student's injury.

▷ Always wear protective gloves when you come in contact with blood, bodily fluids, and torn skin, or when handling materials soiled with the same.

▷ If you come in contact with bodily fluids from a student, throw your gloves away in a lined garbage can. Better yet, seal the soiled gloves in a small plastic bag before depositing them in the trash. After you remove the gloves, wash your hands for 10 seconds with soap and warm running water.

▷ Encourage students to wash their hands before meals and when using the restrooms to reduce exposure to germs.

▷ Do not allow students who are bleeding to participate in class until the bleeding has stopped and the wound has been cleaned and completely covered.

▷ Check with the school office when there is a student injury. Some schools may require you to complete an accident report form. If so, leave a copy for the permanent teacher and keep one for your records.

▷ Prevention is the best antidote for medical emergencies. Always stay with the students. Contact another adult if you need to leave the students at any time. If you have recess duty, walk around the playground and be proactive about potentially dangerous behavior. Remember, you are the adult in charge.

Submitted by Berks County Intermediate Unit, Reading, Pennsylvania

EMERGENCY AND EVACUATION PROCEDURES

- Ask the district office for information about emergency action plans and protocol. Find out what to do in the event of fire, flood, earthquake, bomb threat, etc.

- Since every building and classroom is different, it is important to know where the nearest exit is and have a class list available to grab when you evacuate the building.

- If you hear the fire alarm or a message over the intercom, instruct the students to quickly and quietly leave the room in single file, heading for the designated exit door.

- Some classrooms may have an "emergency backpack" hanging by the door. If you see such a backpack, take it with you when you evacuate.

- After evacuating the building, use the class list to account for all of the students in your class.

Remember:

Be sure to locate and bring a class list with you as you evacuate students. This will help you to make sure all students are accounted for after you leave the building.

For additional downloads, visit:
STEDI.org/ Handbook

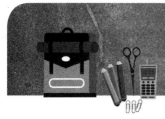

Legal Aspects of the Job

It is important for you to be aware of your legal responsibility in the classroom. As you review these tasks, take the initiative to learn the specifics required of you by the school district.

- **Supervision of Students.** As the substitute teacher, you have physical control of a classroom and a duty to keep students safe and orderly. In many states, a teacher acts "in loco parentis"—in the place of a parent—and is allowed to use her judgment in a manner similar to a parent. Be sure to always maintain a professional standard when it comes to the supervision and safety of the students.

- **Due Care and Caution.** A teacher is required to exercise due care and caution for the safety of the students in his charge. Essentially, this means acting reasonably and with safety in mind, being able to explain circumstances and your actions, and following school safety policies and procedures.

- **Release of Students.** Due to possible restraints on who may have custody of a child, students should not be allowed to leave the building during the school day without express consent from the office.

- **Administering Medication.** Only the school nurse or other health personnel should only administer medication.

- **Confidentiality.** It is unprofessional and against the law in many states to disclose confidential information about your students. Generally, a substitute teacher should avoid comments about individual students that convey private information (e.g., grades, medical condition, learning or discipline problems, etc.).

- **Anecdotal Records.** Maintaining notes on particular incidents in the classroom can protect you in problematic situations. If you feel that a classroom occurrence might be questioned, note the date and time, the individuals involved, the choices for action considered, and the actions taken.

- **Discipline Policies.** You should know the state's position on corporal punishment and the school's policy regarding discipline. Some states require a school to have a policy, and often these policies indicate a specific person, such as the principal, as responsible for disciplinary actions. If in doubt, refer the students to the main office so that you can maintain supervision and due care for the remainder of the class. When sending a student to the principal due to discipline matters, the substitute teacher maintains the duties of supervision and due care for both the individual child and the remainder of the class. For more information on handling discipline problems, review Chapter One of this handbook.

- **Dangerous Situations.** As a substitute teacher you are responsible for making sure the learning environment is safe. This includes tasks such as arranging desks so as not to block exits and properly supervising the use of potentially dangerous classroom equipment. A teacher must also consider the potential for problems in certain kinds of classes. If you feel planned activities in a physical education, science, shop, or home economics class may be unsafe, you may choose to do an alternate activity that you feel can be conducted safely.

> **Remember:**
> *Never leave your students unsupervised.*

Child Abuse Reporting

The purpose of child abuse reporting legislation is to protect the best interests of children, offer protective services to prevent harm to children, stabilize the home environment, preserve family life whenever possible, and encourage cooperation among the states in dealing with the problem of child abuse.

- **Duty to Notify.** School employees (including substitute teachers) who know or reasonably believe that a student has been neglected, or physically or sexually abused, shall immediately notify the building principal, the law enforcement agency, or office of the State Division of Human Services.

- **Further Investigation.** It is not the responsibility of the school employees to prove the student has been abused or neglected. Neither do they need to determine if the student is in need of protection. Investigations are the responsibility of the Division of Human Services. Investigations by education personnel prior to submitting a report should not go beyond simply validating a reasonable belief that a reportable problem exists.

- **Report Suspected Abuse Immediately.** Persons making reports of alleged child abuse or neglect, in good faith, are immune from any civil or criminal liability that might otherwise arise from those actions.

For additional downloads, visit: **STEDI.org/Handbook**

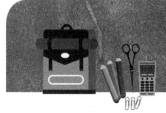

Sexual Harassment

WHAT IS SEXUAL HARASSMENT?

Sexual harassment is defined as unwelcome sexual advances, requests for sexual favors, and other verbal or physical conduct of a sexual nature when:

- submission to such conduct is made, either explicitly or implicitly, a term or condition of a person's employment or a student's academic success
- submission to or rejection of such conduct by an individual is used as the basis for employment or academic decisions affecting such individuals
- such conduct unreasonably interferes with an individual's work or academic performance or creates an intimidating, hostile, or offensive working or learning environment

Sexual harassment can be directed at or perpetrated by you, administrators, faculty members, staff members, or students.

WHAT CONSTITUTES SEXUAL HARASSMENT?

Sexual harassment:
- is unwanted or unwelcome
- is sexual in nature or gender-based
- is severe, pervasive, and/or repeated
- has an adverse impact on the workplace or academic environment
- often occurs in the context of a relationship where one person has more formal power than the other (supervisor/employee, faculty/student, etc.)

Who can I talk to about sexual harassment concerns?

- Your local principal, superintendent, or personnel/human resources office
- Your city or state office of Anti-Discrimination
- Your state office of Equal Employment Opportunity Commission (EEOC)
- The Office of Civil Rights, U.S. Department of Education

OTHER THINGS
YOU SHOULD KNOW

WHAT ARE SOME EXAMPLES OF VERBAL, NONVERBAL, AND PHYSICAL SEXUAL HARASSMENT?

The following are behaviors that could be viewed as sexual harassment when they are unwelcome.

Verbal

- whistling or making cat calls at someone
- making sexual comments about a person's clothing or body
- telling sexual jokes or stories
- referring to an adult woman or man as a hunk, doll, babe, or honey
- spreading rumors about a person's personal sex life
- repeatedly "asking out" a person who is not interested

Nonverbal

- paying unwanted attention to someone (staring, following)
- making facial expressions (winking, throwing kisses, licking)
- making lewd gestures
- giving gifts of a sexual nature

What should I do if I feel I am being sexually harassed?

- Talk to your harasser if possible. Tell her that you find the behavior offensive.
- Continue going to work/classes.
- Document all sexual harassment incidents. Record the time, date, place, and people involved.
- Consider talking to others to see if they have experienced sexual harassment.
- Put your objection in writing, sending a copy by registered mail to the harasser and keeping a copy in your file. Say:
    o On "this date" you did "this."
    o It made me feel "this."
    o I want "this" to happen next (e.g., I want "this" to stop).
- Report the harassment to the building administrator and district personnel/human resource director.

Physical

- hanging around, standing close, or brushing up against a person
- touching a person's clothing, hair, or body
- touching oneself in a sexual manner around another person
- hugging, kissing, patting, stroking, massaging

For additional downloads, visit:
STEDI.org/ Handbook

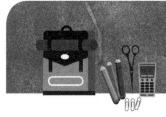

Being Sensitive to Diversity

The United States is home to a diverse population. No other nation enjoys the rich and varied cultural heritages found within our borders. Since this diversity is reflected in our schools, it only makes sense that instructional methods should benefit from, and be sensitive to, the special abilities and needs of people from different groups.

Diversity exists in the classroom in ways that are seen and unseen and is not limited to race and religion. It encompasses differences in cultural traditions and beliefs, the make-up of the family, and the abilities and disabilities of each and every child. Although you will only be in the classroom briefly as a substitute teacher, you still have an obligation to create a classroom environment that is sensitive to diversity. Follow these important reminders as you interact with students and staff:

- Be extremely sensitive when making remarks to students about beliefs, traditions, family, etc. Don't make assumptions.
- Show respect when referring to any race, religion, or culture. Avoid using any slang terms or stereotypes.
- Be quick to point out similarities in students, as we are all more alike than different.
- Be eager and interested in learning about differences in students.
- Enjoy the diversity found among the students in the classes you teach.
- Rather than categorizing students, get to know them as individuals.

For additional downloads, visit: STEDI.org/Handbook

Bullying

According to the U.S. Department of Health and Human Services, the definition of bullying is repeated, unwanted, and aggressive behavior among school-aged children that involve a real or perceived power imbalance. When it comes to bullying behavior, most schools will have a "no tolerance" policy in place.

Many bullying behaviors are obvious, but others are not. As a substitute teacher, it is difficult to track repeated offenses, so we must learn to trust the reaction of students. Even if an infraction seems minor, it is better to err on the side of caution and treat it as if it were a bullying situation. If you see incidents of bullying, intervene by separating the students while remaining calm and modeling how to treat others with respect. Attend to any immediate problems that were caused by the incident and report the misbehavior to a school administrator. You may also consider keeping a record of the incident.

Avoid these common mistakes when responding to bullying:
- Bullying should not be ignored.
- Teachers should respond to bullying incidents immediately; students should feel safe with teachers.
- Avoid feeling as though you need to sort out facts or details of the incident immediately. Instead, wait until later when you can visit with students one-on-one.
- Do not put students into embarrassing situations, because this can make the interaction coercive.
- It is essential that teachers do not become the bully.

Remember, students learn by watching how adults handle situations. When teaching, be sure to model respect while interacting with all students. You can also use "getting to know you" activities to help students see each other as peers.

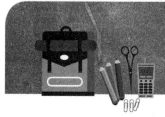

Other Out-of-Classroom Activities

In addition to regular classroom management, there are several special situations that you need to be aware of and prepared for. These situations include assemblies, playground and lunch duty, field trips, bad weather days, and escorting students to the bus. As you review the following suggestions, keep in mind that you are the teacher and must assume full responsibility for all of the students in your care.

Assemblies/Pep Rallies

At first thought, an assembly may seem like a pleasant break in the school day routine. However, it can turn into a nightmare for a substitute teacher who does not have a plan for managing students during this activity. Here are some suggestions to help you survive the event with nerves still intact.

- Find out the time and location of the assembly, and whether or not the students will need to bring chairs from the classroom.

- Check to see how the regular class schedule will be altered to accommodate the assembly.

- Talk to neighboring teachers to find out specific procedures for going to and returning from an assembly, as well as assigned seating for each class.

- If there are no established procedures, plan your own (walk in a single file line down the hall to the assembly, sit together as a class, return in a single file line, etc.).

- Determine and explain the specific behavior you expect during the assembly, and review the consequences and rewards that will follow meeting the expectations.

- Avoid punishing the whole class for the misdeeds of a few, which can frustrate students and add to discipline problems.

Field Trips

Field trips give students first-hand learning opportunities and are often used to introduce or conclude a specific topic of study. You have many duties in order to successfully carry out the planned learning experience when substituting on the day of a field trip.

- Parental permission to participate in the field trip must be secured prior to the trip. Be certain that every student in the class has turned in a signed release/consent form.

- Find out the school policy for any students who do not have documented parental permission to participate in the field trip. If a student without permission is required to remain at school, arrange for him to attend another teacher's class.

Do	Don´t
• Be courteous	• Ask personal or irrelevant questions
• Stay with the group	• Lag behind
• Listen attentively	• Interrupt
• Follow safety rules	• Take samples or touch, unless given specific permission to do so

Special Duties and Responsibilities

Your assignment as a substitute teacher may include additional responsibilities such as hall, lunch, or bus duty. Specific instructions associated with such an assignment should be explained by the principal/ secretary or outlined in the permanent teacher's lesson plans. If not, keep the following in mind:

- Supervisory duties involve more than just being near the students. Your job is to supervise student actions and activities to ensure a safe environment and experience.
- Be proactive in managing potential problem situations. Your active presence is usually enough to discourage inappropriate behavior.
    - Be alert and attentive to what students are doing.
    - Remain standing.
    - Move about the area you are supervising as much as possible.
- Should a problem arise, intervene before the situation gets out of control, and don't hesitate to ask for help from another teacher.
- Never leave a group of students unsupervised.

In Conclusion

There are very few "normal" school days in a classroom. Fire drills seem to occur at the least convenient times. In addition, assemblies alter usual routines; field trips, epidemics, and school competitions often result in large numbers of students being absent. Plus, simply the fact that you are there as a substitute teacher means that it is not a "normal" day for the students in your classes.

Knowledge, flexibility, and a sense of humor are key to making the best out of any situation. Learn all that you can about school policies, procedures, and responsibilities. Recognize that things will rarely go exactly as you or the permanent teacher have planned and be prepared to make accommodations. If you lighten up and laugh, including at yourself, then it will make for a much better day for everyone.

*A*s a substitute teacher, it can be difficult to see the big picture and how a particular assignment fits into the teacher's overall plan. However, the permanent teacher is counting on you to help students complete the work they've assigned and keep the class on track. Extra fill-in activities you bring should be used only when the assigned work is completed or when there is a particular reason that you are unable to carry out the lesson plan.

You will also run into situations when the permanent teacher has not been able to leave plans, when the plans are impossible to decipher, or when activities run too short. These situations leave you with the challenge of filling class time with manageable and worthwhile activities. Every substitute teacher should have some "tried and true" activities to keep in his **SubPack** that can keep students occupied and learning at the same time.

Consider photocopying enough handouts for an average size class before you get to the school. This will allow you to have time to review the lesson plan and prepare a starter activity before the students arrive. After the school day is over make copies to replenish your supplies.

Try introducing filler activities as a normal part of the lesson by saying something like, *"When you finish answering the questions found in chapter two, I have a fun activity for you to work on with another person. It will be found here on the teacher's desk."* This helps you avoid a discussion about whether or not the activity is for credit. Make sure the activities you choose are fun and engaging so students will want to complete them.

This chapter will introduce you to four types of filler activities:
- Starter Activities
- Five-Minute Filler Activities
- Short Activities
- Early-Finisher Activities

Remember:
Fill-in activities are meant to supplement, not replace the permanent teacher's lesson plan.

Tips for Using Fill-In Activities

Each of the activities found in this chapter and online has a suggested time requirement, but feel free to adjust as needed.

The activities are also organized into categories but understand that many activities can be adapted to fit other content areas.

Consider letting students work in groups or independently and then together for the last few minutes, which encourages students to stay engaged but also allows for some socializing.

The teaching strategies from Chapter Two can also be beneficial when implementing fill-in activities. For example, use a Lesson Kickstarter when you want to help students get into gear before a lesson.

If you don't have the time or resources to photocopy worksheets, you can still complete the activity by reading the questions aloud and allowing students to respond.

Allow enough time to check answers or share results at the end of an activity or assignment. If this is not possible, leave an answer key with the permanent teacher for students to check their work the next day.

You can provide answers in several different ways:
- Read them aloud at the end of the activity.
- Tape the answer key to a desk or wall for students to check.
- Answer keys can be photocopied and distributed when students finish the assignment.

It is important to always evaluate student work before returning it to them. Even a couple of words at the top of the page recognizes their effort and validates the worth of the assignment.

If you use handouts from your **SubPack**, ask to use the photocopy machine in the office to replenish your supply.

Many of the activities and lessons in this chapter include adaptations for students with special needs and accelerated learners, which are indicated by the icons shown here. Additional suggestions for adapting activities to meet the needs of all learners are found in Chapters Four and Five.

This chapter details several fill-in activities but you can log in at STEDI.org/Handbook to access 150 more! Check back often because STEDI.org will be working to increase the pool of activities that you print and use in your next class.

Starter Activities

As discussed in Chapter One, starter activities are crucial for substitute teachers. Many permanent teachers leave instructions for a starter activity, but if an activity isn't left, following are a few ideas. For additional starter activities, visit **STEDI.org/Handbook.**

For the
Permanent Teacher

GRADE LEVELS 1-8

Time:	5-10 minutes
Objective:	Students will write a thank you note to their permanent teacher and start working immediately.
Materials:	Paper and pencil for each student
Procedures:	1. Write on the whiteboard: Take out a blank sheet of paper and write a thank you letter to your teacher. Include three things that you like about him or her and why. The letter should be at least three paragraphs long.
	2. Collect the letters and leave them for the permanent teacher.

Favorite Lyrics
or Quote

GRADE LEVELS 6-12

Time:	5 minutes
Objective:	Students will write about their favorite lyrics or quote and start working immediately.
Materials:	Paper and pencil for each student
Procedures:	1. Write on the whiteboard: What is your favorite song or quote that you've heard? Why? What experiences have you had in your life that caused you to connect with the song/quote? Please write at least two paragraphs to explain.
	2. Have students share their essays with another student in the class.

Starters

Would you Rather...

- Would you rather drink a gallon of ketchup or mustard? Why?

- Would you rather have a panda or anteater as a pet? Why?

- Would you rather have one extra toe or one less finger? Why?

- Would you rather always have to ride your bike wherever you go or ride the bus? Why?

- Would you rather always have to say everything that came to your mind or never speak again? Why?

- Would you rather be able to fly or be invisible? Why?

- Would you rather be able to hear any conversation or take back anything you say? Why?

- Would you rather love and not be loved back, or be loved but never love? Why?

- Would you rather publish your diary or make a movie about your most embarrassing moment? Why?

- Would you rather be rich and ugly, or good-looking and poor?

- Would you rather go on a one week trip to a foreign country of your choice or take a four week trip around your own country? Why?

- Would you rather get $1000 right now or $50 a month for the rest of your life? Why?

- Would you rather have bright pink teeth or bright pink hair? Why?

- Would you rather have three eyes or two noses? Why?

- Would you rather always have your nose plugged or always have your ears plugged? Why?

- Would you rather have your friends be smarter than you or better looking? Why?

- Would you rather sing every word you speak or always speak in rhymes? Why?

- Would you rather spend every minute of the rest of your life indoors or outdoors? Why?

- Would you rather have to learn to walk all over again or learn to write all over again? Why?

- Would you rather have to get everywhere by crawling or stand on your hands when you are stationary? Why?

If you could only...

- If you could only eat one breakfast cereal for the rest of your life, which would it be? Why?

- If you could only eat at one restaurant for the rest of your life, which would it be? Why?

- If you could only have one super power, what would it be? Why?

- If you could be one movie character, who it would it be? Why?

- If you were an animal, which animal would you be? Why?

- If you could only read one book for the rest of your life, which would it be? Why?

- If you could only watch one TV series for the rest of your life, which would it be? Why?

- If you could have lunch with one person from history, who would it be? Why?

- If you could change your name, what would you change it to? Why?

- If you could go back and change one event in history, which would it be? Why?

- Do you think crying is a sign of weakness or strength? Why?

- If you could only have one hobby, what would it be? Why?

- What is your happiest childhood memory? What makes it so special?

- How would you like to be remembered? What are you doing to ensure that legacy?

Draw any of the following emotions:

Happy	Lonely
Sad	Discouraged
Angry	Cowardly
Joy	Humility
Shyness	Stingy
Curious	Moody
Grief-stricken	Selfish
Stressed	Fearless

Anagrams

See how many words you can create from any one of the following:

Alphabets	Friend
Aluminum	Grease
Amazingly	Heredity
Apartment	Mobbed
Beware	Oceans
Bowling	Starting
Brownie	Strawberry
Crayon	

Secret Message

For each letter of the alphabet, create a symbol. Then write a message in your new alphabet for someone to decode.

Story Chart

Time:	10 minutes
Objective:	Students will complete a creative writing assignment and start working as soon as they walk into the classroom.
Materials:	Pencil and paper for each student
Procedures:	1. Draw the following chart on the white board:

WRITE A:	ABOUT:		
• Commercial	• An old	• Man	• Who finds a treasure map
• Newspaper article	• A young	• Lady	• Who makes a new friend
• Letter	• A silly	• Bunny	• Who wins a race
• A day in the life of	• An angry	• Snake	• Who gets a new job
• Horror story	• A nerdy	• Car	• Who builds a tree house
			• Who goes swimming

2. Tell students to select any combination from the chart above. They have ten minutes to complete the writing assignment.
3. Select a few volunteers to read their stories aloud to the class.

TIPS FOR Success: *If it's appropriate for the age level, you may want to consider encouraging students to write at least three paragraphs.*

Writing Prompts

GRADE LEVELS 2-12

Time:	5–45 minutes
Materials Needed:	Paper, pencil
Objective:	Students will practice writing and editing skills.
Advance Preparation:	Select a writing prompt for the students. Create a handout, write it on the board, or be prepared to give it verbally.

This activity can fill five minutes or an entire lesson depending on the complexity of the writing prompt, and at which step you want students to stop work and turn in their work for teacher evaluation. There are no right or wrong answers, rather, writing prompts provide an opportunity for students to explore their own thoughts, values, and beliefs. Encourage students to explain and justify their responses. Do not allow students to criticize the thoughts and opinions of others. |
| **Procedures:** | 1. Provide the class with a writing prompt and time limit for completing the first draft of their work.
2. Get students to exchange papers and edit one another's work for content and technical components.
3. Allow students time to discuss their editorial comments with one another, and get a second opinion from other students, if time permits.
4. After the editing process, get students to complete a second draft of their work and hand it in for teacher evaluation. |
| **Writing Prompts:** | A. Write an invitation to a social event, real or imaginary, formal or casual.
B. Write a letter to a national news agency convincing them to cover a recent or upcoming event at your school.
C. Write a menu for a new restaurant in town.
D. Write a chronological report of everything you have done so far today.
E. Write an outline of your life. Include events you anticipate will happen in the future.
G. Write a brief essay about what life as a street light would be like.
H. Write a description of eating ice cream. |

Writing Prompts:	I. Write an evaluation of the pen or pencil you are using. J. Write a memo to your boss asking him/her for a raise. K. Write a synopsis of a book you have recently read. L. Write a newspaper article about current fashion trends or a recent sporting event. M. If this weekend you could do anything you wanted to, what would you do? N. If you were a teacher and the students in your class wouldn't stop talking what would you do? What if you did that and they still didn't stop talking? O. If there was a poster competition coming up, would you rather create a poster all by yourself and get all of the credit, or work with a group and share the credit with the other group members? P. If you could be invisible for one day, what would you do? Q. If your parents were going to be living in a foreign country for the next year, would you rather go with them or stay in your own neighborhood with a friend? Why? R. What would the perfect day at school be like? S. If you could change just one thing about school, what would you change? T. Pretend you could only have one pair of shoes for the next year. Would you choose shoes that are really comfortable but look kind of goofy, or shoes that look really cool but are uncomfortable to wear? U. What are two things you don't like now, but ten years from now you don't think will be so bad? V. What subjects in school do you think are really important to study? Why? W. If you could pick any age, and be that age for the rest of your life, what age would you want to be? Why? X. If you could choose new jobs for your parents, what would you choose and why?
Adapting for Students with Special Needs:	• ***Write fewer sentences.*** • ***Use more time to complete the assignment.*** • ***Refer to a list of key words to use.***

Five-Minute Filler Activities

This type of filler activity uses critical thinking to keep the class involved during the spare moments that occur throughout the day, such as the last five minutes before lunch, or to get everyone refocused after break time. Students can complete Five-Minute Filler activities independently, in groups, or as a whole class. Several different types of these quick, engaging activities are explained below to help you introduce, enhance, or compliment the lesson for the day.

Act It Out

GRADE LEVELS K-12

Time:	10 minutes
Objective:	Assess student understanding through kinesthetic methods.
Materials Needed:	Key words for the lesson written on strips of paper
Procedures:	1. Write key words on strips of paper and place in a hat or bowl. 2. Choose a student to select a paper from the pile and instruct them to act out (or play charades to) the word on their paper. 3. See how many words the class can guess before class ends.

TIPS FOR Success: *It may be necessary to explain the techniques for playing charades such as how many words are in the phrase, whether it's an action/person/place, which word they are acting out first, etc. Try not to split the class into teams to compete with each other, but rather have them compete against the clock and work together. This will make classroom management easier.*

Classroom
Cartoons

Time:	15 minutes
Objective:	Student will summarize and apply the lessons learned in class through drawings.
Materials Needed:	Sample cartoon strip Pencils Strips of paper for each student (8 ½ x 11 cut lengthwise)
Procedures:	1. Show students your sample cartoon strip. 2. Tell students they are to create a cartoon strip of their own showing what they learned in class today. 3. If it's easier, students can base their cartoon around the skill they have learned in class, or the knowledge in action. 4. Give students 10 minutes (or less depending on the lesson topic) to complete their cartoon strips. 5. When students have completed their drawings, have them exchange cartoons several times with other classmates so that others can see their creation. (Bonus: students are reinforcing their knowledge over and over without even realizing it!)

TIPS FOR Success: *For students who do not feel confident in their drawing abilities, assure them that stick figures and simple sketches are great, and that the content and ideas behind the cartoon are most important.*

Don't Drop
the Ball

GRADE LEVELS K-12

Time:	5–10 minutes
Objective:	Assess student understanding of the day's lesson
Materials Needed:	Object to toss to students such as bean bag, inflatable beach ball, etc. List of review questions
Procedures:	1. Have students remain seated or sit in a circle if the classroom set up allows. 2. Throw an inflatable ball around the room and ask a question mid-air. 3. Whoever catches the object must attempt to answer the question. 4. If the student answers the question correctly, they can throw the object to another student and ask a different question mid-air. 5. If the student answers the question incorrectly, they throw the object back to the substitute. 6. Repeat as many times as necessary.

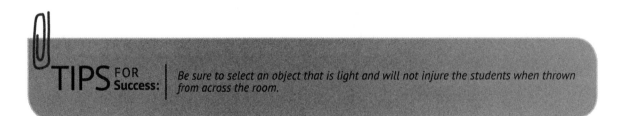

TIPS FOR Success: *Be sure to select an object that is light and will not injure the students when thrown from across the room.*

Five Finger
Facts

Time:	5–10 minutes
Objective:	Learning each other's names and something about them.
Materials Needed:	Paper Pencil

Procedures:	1. Have each student trace his or her hand on a piece of paper.
	2. Print their names in the middle of the handprint.
	3. In each of the fingers write a fact about themselves.
	
	    a. Things they did today.
	    b. Things they like to eat.
	    c. Things they like to do.
	    d. Things they like to play.
	    e. Thinks they like to listen to.
	
	4. Either pass the hands around or read them as a group.

TIPS FOR Success: | *Encourage students to write something that is specific to them.*

Getting Students
to Line Up

Following are some suggestions for getting students lined up at the door. To make things a little more fun, you may want to time the students to see how fast they can do it.

- Line up in alphabetical order by first or last name.
- Line up in order of birthday starting in January.
- Line up in height order, shortest to tallest.

For a little variety, you may want to try one of the following ways.

Line up if you can tell me:

- The name of a country and its capital.
- A kind of grain.
- A type of tree.
- A type of cloud.
- An animal that is found in the wetlands, on a farm, in the jungle, etc.
- A type of flower.
- One thing you learned at school today.
- A mode of transportation

Line up if you have:

- A tooth missing.
- Khaki pants on.
- Been to the emergency room.
- Participated in a play.
- A dog, cat, mouse…
- A "Z" in your name, an "M"….
- Helped your parents mow the lawn, cleaned the kitchen, washed the car, etc.
- Sneakers, flip-flops, boots, etc.
- Stood on your head, done a cartwheel, ran a mile…

If I
Were A...

GRADE LEVELS
K-4

Time:	Varied
Objective:	To keep students engaged in an activity.
Procedures:	This activity can be done while students are sitting in their desks or waiting in line. Have students complete any of the following statements: • *"If I were a food, I would be..."* • *"If I were a sport, I would be..."* • *"If I were a plant, I would be..."* • *"If I were an animal, I would be..."* • *"If I were a season, I would be..."* • *"If I were a dinosaur, I would be..."*

Number
Phrases

GRADE LEVELS
4-8

Time:	Varied
Procedures:	Copy one or more of the abbreviated phrases below on the board and challenge students to guess the phrase (see answers below).

		ANSWERS:	
A.	26 - L. of the A.	A.	26 letters of the alphabet
B.	7 - W. of the W.	B.	7 wonders of the world
C.	54 - C. in a D. (with the J.)	C.	54 cards in a deck (with the Jokers)
D.	88 - P. K.	D.	88 piano keys
E.	18 - H. on a G. C.	E.	18 holes on a golf course
F.	90 - D. in a R. A.	F.	90 degrees in a right angle
G.	4 - Q. in a G.	G.	4 quarts in a gallon
H.	24 - H. in a D.	H.	24 hours in a day
I.	11 - P. on a F. T.	I.	11 players on a football team
J.	29 - D. in F. in a L. Y.	J.	29 days in February in a Leap Year
K.	76 - T. L. the B. P.	K.	76 trombones lead the big parade
L.	20,000 - L. U. T. S.	L.	20,000 leagues under the sea
M.	7 - D. of the W.	M.	7 days of the week
N.	12 - E. in a D.	N.	12 eggs in a dozen
O.	3 - B. M. (S. H. T. R.!)	O.	3 blind mice (see how they run!)

Sponge
Activities

If you have just a few minutes, consider implementing one of these activities. Either brainstorm answers as a class, or have students create lists individually.

- List all the objects in the classroom that weigh less than 5 grams.

- List all of the objects in the room that weigh more than one kilogram.

- List all the objects in the classroom that would sink in water.

- List all of the objects in the classroom that would float in water.

- List all of the objects in the classroom that would be attracted to a magnet.

- List all of the objects in the classroom that would conduct electricity.

- List all of the objects in the classroom that are electrical insulators.

- List words that begin with the letter T, R, S, or D.

- List all of the ways you help your parents.

- List foods you like.

- List all of the places you'd like to visit.

- List all of the books you've read.

- List all of the movies you've seen.

- List all of the cereals you can think of.

- List all of the desserts you can think of.

- List things you love to do in the winter/summer/spring/fall.

- List all of the places you find sand.

- List as many love songs as you can think of.

- List all the forms of transportation you can think of.

- List all of the different types of musical instruments you can.

- List the states that have the letter "e" in their name.

- Write down a manufactured product for every letter of the alphabet.

- List as many different individual and/or team sports as you can.

- List as many states as you can.

- List as many colors as you can.

- List as many pets as you can.

- List as many types of flowers as you can.

- List as many jungle animals as you can.

- List as many countries as you can.

Quick
Five-Minute Filler

Grade Levels:	Adjustable
Time:	Varied
Objective:	To keep the students engaged until the final bell rings.
Materials:	As Needed
Procedures:	The last five or ten minutes of class can be the most difficult time to keep students on task. Often times the lesson plan ends early so you can be prepared with an activity that will keep students focused and prevent potential problems. Here are some examples of prompts that could be used to keep students on task. The activity works well when completed as a class, by individual students, or by small groups of students. • Write down all of the places you find sand. • List as many love songs as you can think of. • List all the forms of transportation you can think of. • Name all of the different types of musical instruments you can. • List the states that have the letter "e" in their name. • Write down a manufactured product for every letter of the alphabet. • Name as many different individual and/or team sports as you can.

TIPS FOR Success: *These lists can be created verbally or written down. You can add interest and motivation to the activity by setting a time limit, challenging students to come up with a specific number of answers, or by tallying which student/group has the most original answers.*

Early-Finisher Activities

In every class, there will be several students who finish their assignments early. With nothing to do, even "good" students may behave inappropriately and disrupt the work of the whole class. The following sample activities are designed to keep early finishers involved in constructive activities and motivate the class to work hard so they can participate in these fun activities. As you select activities to use as Early Finishers, remember to adjust each activity to the situation and individual needs of students.

At the Back
of the Room

- Set up a puzzle that students can work on throughout the day.
- Set up a reading corner where students can go and read silently after they have finished an assignment.
- Have kits prepared of Tangram puzzles that students can access after completing an assignment (found at **STEDI.org/Handbook)**.

All About Me

Name: ....

- Draw a picture of your family.

- Write the names of four friends in your class.

  ....

  ....

- Draw three clocks showing:

  - when you got up.

  - when you eat lunch.

  - when you go to bed.

- Draw a car using only circles.

- Write the numbers counting by 5's to 50.

  ....

  ....

- Write a sentence using six words that start with the letter B.

  ....

  ....

- Make a list of everything you ate yesterday.

  ....

  ....

  ....

  ....

  ....

- Close your eyes. Listen! Write down six things you hear.

  ....

  ....

  ....

  ....

- What is your favorite color? List five things that color.

  ....

  ....

  ....

  ....

  ....

- Write down 10 things you would like to get for your birthday.

  ....

  ....

  ....

  ....

  ....

- If you were the teacher what would you do?

  ....

  ....

- Write the numbers backwards from 25 to 0.

  ....

  ....

- Write down seven things that start with the same letter as your first name.

  ....

  ....

- Draw an animal using only triangles.

- Write down five things you will use today that start with the letter T.

  ....

  ....

  ....

  ....

- How old are you?

  ....

- If you smiled at everyone you saw for one whole day, what do you think would happen?

  ....

- Write the days of the week.

  ....

  ....

  ....

  ....

- What is your favorite animal?

  ....

- If you could do anything you wanted, what would you do today?

  ....

If History Were Altered

Name: ....

How would the world be different today if the colonists had not won the Revolutionary War and the new country had remained under British rule?

....
....
....
....
....

How would the world be different today if electricity had never been invented?

....
....
....
....
....

How would the world be different today if the atomic bomb had not been used against the Japanese in World War II?

....
....
....
....
....

How would the world be different today if Columbus and his ships had perished at sea and never reached the American Continents?

....
....
....
....
....

How would the world be different today if travel by airplane had never been developed?

....
....
....
....
....

Brain Teasers
and Riddles

GRADE LEVELS 3-8

1. What is full of holes, yet holds water? *A sponge*

2. What is bought by the yard, yet worn by the foot? *Carpet*

3. What is the longest word in the English language? *Smiles. There is a mile between the first and last letter.*

4. If eight birds are on a roof and you shoot at one, how many remain? *None. They all fly away.*

5. Why can't it rain for two days continually? *Because there is always a night in between.*

6. What speaks every language? *An echo*

7. Why is a nose in the middle of a face? *Because it is the scenter.*

8. What table is completely without legs? *A time-table*

9. What is the difference between a jeweller and a jailer? One sells watches, the other watches cells.

10. What is black and white and read all over? *A newspaper.*

11. Can a man living in Chicago be buried west of the Mississippi? *No. He is still alive.*

12. How far can a dog run into the woods? *Halfway. The other half he is running out.*

13. A farmer had seventeen sheep. All but nine died. How many did he have left? *Nine.*

14. A man has two coins in his hand. The two coins total thirty cents. One is not a nickel. What are the two coins? *A nickel and a quarter. (The other is a nickel.)*

15. Why is Ireland the wealthiest country? *Because its capital is always Dublin.*

16. If a telephone and a piece of paper had a race, who would always win? *The telephone, since the paper will always remain stationery.*

17. Why should fish be well-educated? *They are found in schools.*

18. Which takes the least amount of time to get ready for a trip: An elephant or a rooster? *The rooster... He only takes his comb, but the elephant has to take a whole trunk.*

19. Do they have a Fourth of July in England? *Yes. (But it is not a holiday.)*

20. Take two apples from three apples. What have you got? *Two apples.*

21. Four men can build four boats in four days. How long will it take one man to build one boat? *Four days. (Four men building four boats is the same as one man working sixteen days.)*

22. Can you measure out exactly two gallons of water using only two unmarked containers, one of the containers will hold eight gallons and the other will hold five gallons? *Pour five gallons into the eight gallon can. Then repeat this until the eight gallon can is full. (Two gallons remain in the five gallon can.)*

Mind
Benders

GRADE LEVELS 4-8

1. The Shopping Trip

One day last week my brother went to town with only $10 in his pocket, but returned in the evening with $20.

He bought a pair of shoes at a sporting goods store and some meat at the meat market. He also had his eyes examined. It so happens that my brother gets paid every Thursday by check and the banks in this town are open on Tuesday, Friday, and Saturday only. The eye doctor is not in his office on Saturday and there is no market on Thursday and Friday. What day did my brother go to town?

2. The Chess Tournament Dilemma

Four men named P.F. Smith, C.J. Smith, Reynolds, and Fellows played in a chess tournament.

The Smiths were the famous Smith brothers, twins who played opposite ends on the Princeton football team.

Reynolds surprised everyone when he defeated Fellows.

The man who finished third said graciously to the winner at the conclusion of the matches, "I've heard a great deal about you and I am happy to meet you. May I congratulate you?"

The runner-up was unable to walk, having had infantile paralysis when he was four years old. He had never married, but had lived a sheltered life with his widowed mother, making chess his chief diversion.

P.F. Smith sometimes talked too much. He had disgraced himself when he was an usher at Fellow's wedding by making the bride's mother late for the wedding.

In what order did the men finish the chess tournament?

3. The Artisans

There are three men, named James, John, and Jake, each of whom is engaged in two occupations. Their jobs classify each of them as two of the following: chauffeur, electrician, musician, painter, gardener, and barber. From the following facts, find in what two occupations each man is engaged.

1. The chauffeur offended the musician by laughing at his long hair.
2. Both the musician and the gardener used to go fishing with James.
3. The painter had the electrician wire his new house.
4. The chauffeur dated the painter's sister.
5. John owed the gardener $5.00.
6. J ake beat both John and the painter at horseshoes.

4. The Stolen Antique

Three men, Mr. White, Mr. Black and Mr. Brown and their wives were entertained at the home of their friend one evening. After the departure of the guests, the host and hostess discovered that a valuable antique had been stolen. It was later discovered that one of the six guests was the thief. From the facts given, see if you can discover who it was.

1. The spouse of the thief lost money at cards that evening.
2. Because of partial paralysis of his hands and arms, Mr. Brown was unable to drive his car.
3. Mrs. Black and another female guest spent the entire evening doing a jigsaw puzzle.
4. Mr. Black accidentally spilled a drink on Mrs. White when he was introduced to her.
5. Mr. Brown gave his wife half of the money that he had won to make up for her loss.
6. Mr. Black had beaten the thief at golf that day.

Solutions to Mind Benders:

1. The Shopping Trip
My brother went to town on Tuesday.

2. Chess Tournament Dilemma
Winner-C.J. Smith;
Runner-up- Reynolds;
Third- Fellows;
Fourth- P.F. Smith

3. The Artisans
James- barber and painter;
John- musician and electrician
Jake- chauffeur and gardener

4. The Stolen Antique
Mrs. Black was the thief.

Name
Poetry

GRADE LEVELS 2-8

Time:	15–30 minutes
Materials Needed:	• Pencil • Paper
Advance Preparation:	Create an example of a Name Poem to used as you teach this activity.
Objective:	Students will create a poem that is an expression of their own traits and personal characteristics.

Procedures:	1. Discuss different types of poetry. Ask students to share some poems that are familiar to them.
	2. Tell the students that today they are going to create a poem about themselves.
	3. Demonstrate an example of a Name Poem (acrostic poem) on the board.
	
	    Example:
	    C is for chocolate chip cookies, which are my favorite
	    Y is for the yellow flowers that grow in my garden
	    N is for Nika my cat
	    T is for the tree house I helped build
	    H is for happy thoughts
	    I is for ice-cream on my birthday
	    A is for all of the other things that make up me
	
	4. Ask the students to make a name poem using their own name.
	5. Share the name poems with the class or in small groups.
	6. Collect the poems for teacher evaluation and display.

Extension:	Create Acrostic Poems using other topics such as holidays, school subjects, sports, etc. Illustrate the poems by drawing and coloring pictures of the things described in the poem.

Make it More Challenging

- Make the poem rhyme.
- Use first and last name.
- Use 20 descriptive words (adjectives).

TIPS FOR Success: *Younger students may have difficulty in completing this assignment with only one example for instruction. It may be helpful to create a second poem on the board, as a class, before they write their own.*

Riddle
Poems

GRADE LEVELS
K-6

Time:	5 Minutes
Objective:	Students will review the following poems and try to determine what classroom item it is referring to.
Materials Needed:	None
Procedures:	1. Read the following riddle poems to students and ask them to point to the item in the classroom when they know what it is. I have two hands. I have a face. My hands go round and round. I have the numbers 1-12 instead of the smiles and frowns. Find me in the classroom. **Answer: Clock** I have four legs. I'm made from a tree. You stuff your books inside of me. Find me the in the classroom. **Answer: Desk** I'm a yellow fellow with a pointed head. As thin as thin can be. But I leave a trail on a blank white page when someone writes with me. **Answer: Pencil** I'm covered with lines and I'm most often white. I'm handy when you want to write. **Answer: Paper** I take your books from home to school. I'm red or blue or green or black. You zip my zippers here and there. I'm always riding piggyback. **Answer: Backpack**

I'm rainbow colors like red and blue.
When you draw or color, I'm what you use.
Answer: Crayon

Over my head and under my feet,
The rope twirls around, as I jump to the beat.
What am I doing?
Answer: Jumping rope

I'm "it." I chase you – one, two, three.
I try to catch the friends I see.
What am I doing?
Answer: Playing tag

I climb the ladder then I sit down.
Whoosh! I'm swishing to the ground!
Answer: Slide

Word
Puzzles

	se ar ch an d	NEFRIENDED	wear —— long
E R A KISS M			
egsg gesg segg sgeg	S M O K E	GIVE GET GIVE GET GIVE GET GIVE GET	cover agent
NOT GUILTY STANDER	man —— board	EZ iiii	LM AL EA AE EM ML

BELT
——
HITTING
	A
	    S D
	    L
	        A
		he {art	T. V.

ar up ms	CHAIR	TIRE	T O W N

I SOCK	1,000 1 000	COSTS	ground / feet feet / feet feet / feet feet
go i / g n o / a r o / d n u	time time	stand / I	TOUCH
standing / miss FRIENDS	WALKING	SOUP	ter very esting
r e a d i n g	b sick ed	LO head / heels VE	knee / lights
g r u / the block / n i n n	everyrightthing	R R / O O / A / D D / S S	i / 8

Answers to Word Puzzles

Word Puzzles One:

1. Kiss and make up
2. Search high and low
3. Friend in need
4. Long underwear
5. Scrambled eggs
6. Up in smoke
7. Forgive and forget
8. Undercover agent
9. Innocent bystander
10. Man overboard
11. Easy on the eyes
12. Three square meals
13. Hitting below the belt
14. Tossed salad
15. Broken heart
16. Black and white TV
17. Up in arms
18. High chair
19. Flat tire
20. Downtown

Word Puzzles Two:

1. Sock in the eye
2. One in a million
3. Rising costs
4. Six feet underground
5. Going around in circles
6. Time after time
7. I understand
8. Touchdown
9. Misunderstanding between friends
10. Walking tall
11. Split pea soup
12. Very interesting
13. Reading between the lines
14. Sick in bed
15. Head over hills in love
16. Neon lights
17. Running around the block
18. Right in the middle of everything
19. Crossroads
20. I over ate

Minute
Mysteries

Minute Mysteries are stories that are told within a minute and then require the listeners to solve a mystery. Students generate questions that can be answered with a simple "yes" or "no" in order to solve the mystery. These stories are fun and teach children to use critical thinking skills while they sort through the information to work out the answer.

1. A cowboy left town on Tuesday and was gone three days, coming back on Tuesday.
   Q. How is that possible?
   A. His horse was named Tuesday.

2. A man is found dead in a cabin in the ocean.
   Q. What could have happened?
   A. The man is in the cabin of an airplane that crashed into the ocean.

3. A person lived on the 15th floor of a high-rise building. Everyday he got into the elevator, rode down to the lobby and went to work. Every evening he came home from work, took the elevator to the 13th floor and walked up the stairs to his apartment.
   Q. Why?
   A. The person is very short and can only reach the elevator button to the 13th floor.

4. A man was lonely and wanted a talking parrot to keep him company. He went to the pet shop and found a beautiful bird that was for sale at a bargain price. He asked the shop owner if the bird could be trained to talk. The owner said, *"This bird is absolutely guaranteed to repeat everything it hears."* So the man bought the bird and took it home. But two weeks later he returned to the shop, demanding his money back, saying, *"The bird refused to talk."* The shop owner said, *"I stand by my guarantee and will not give your money back."*
   Q. How could he say that, considering the bird wouldn't talk?
   A. The parrot was deaf.

Writing for an Audience

GRADE LEVELS 4-12

Time:	15–30 minutes
Materials Needed:	Pencil Paper A classroom object
Advance Preparation:	Make a list of potential audiences and purposes for writing on the chalkboard (see examples below).
Objective:	Students will practice writing for different audiences.
Procedures:	1. Hold up a common object in the classroom (ruler, stapler, key, tablet, etc.). 2. Discuss what the object is and what it is used for. 3. Ask the students to choose an audience and purpose for writing from the board. Give the students a time limit and have them write about the object discussed in procedure 2. 4. Instruct students to not tell anyone the audience they have selected. 5. Get volunteers to read their paragraphs aloud and get the class members to guess which audience they selected. **Examples of Audiences and Purposes:** • Tell a story about the object in procedure 1 to a Kindergarten class. • Write in a diary as though you were an archeologist who dug up this object two hundred years from now. • You are from another planet and you are writing home to explain how the object is used on Earth. • Write a memo to the principal explaining why this object should be purchased for every student in the school. • Explain to someone who has never seen this object how it is used. • Write specific details about this object so that the reader could walk into the classroom and pick it out from other similar objects.
Extension:	Get students to select another object in the classroom and write about it without mentioning it by name. Trade papers among class members and have them try to work out what object the person is writing about.

| **For Students with Special Needs:** | • *Provide hints or suggestions about what audience to write for.*
• *Have student dictate their story to a scribe.* |

TIPS FOR **Success:**

Setting specific guidelines for the writing assignment will help with this activity. Specify that it should be at least five sentences or that ten minutes will be all the time available for writing. The younger the students, the more specific instructions they will need.

Establishing guessing procedures for step five will help with classroom management. Students will want to call out their guesses as the volunteers read their paragraphs. Establish that no one is to guess until the reader has read their entire paper and that the reader will call on someone who has raised his/her hand when s/he has finished.

Short Activities

Unexpected events or insufficient lesson plans may occasionally leave you with extra class time. You can be prepared by having a short activity ready that the entire class can participate in. These activities are usually directed by the teacher and can range from 20 to 40 minutes.

Samples are explained below with additional Short Activities included in the Activities section of this chapter. Some examples include extensions to use for early finishers and extra class time.

Poster Creation
Review

GRADE LEVELS K-8

Subjet:	Adaptable
Time:	30+ minutes
Materials:	pencil, paper, crayons and other art supplies
Objective:	Students will create a poster that reflects something they have learned in a recent lesson.
Procedures:	1. Review concepts or ideas that students have studied in a lesson that day. 2. List these concepts and ideas on the board. 3. Set a time limit for the posters to be completed. 4. Have students create a poster depicting some aspect of the lesson. 5. Collect posters for the teacher to evaluate and display in the classroom.
Extension:	Have volunteers explain their posters to the class.

The
Newspaper

GRADE LEVELS K-12

Subject:	Language Arts
Time:	15–30 minutes
Materials Needed:	newspaper pencil paper
Objective:	Apply real-life examples to learning that occurs in the classroom.

Procedures:	The newspaper can be a lifesaver when substitute teaching. If there are no plans, the newspaper can be used to teach anything!
	
	• In a kindergarten class, students can circle letters of the alphabet to learn upper and lower case concepts.
	• In first grade, students could circle words they recognize or discuss the emotions depicted in pictures.
	• Students at various grade levels can:
	  • create a shopping list from ads and use math skills to create a total cost
	  • forecast weather and discuss climate
	  • work out statistics for sporting events
	  • write a classified ad or cartoon to expand writing skills to different audiences
	  • create a budget using data from job opportunities, apartment rental, and food advertisement sections

Compare A Plant
Cell to Your School

Teacher Directions:

On the following page students are to compare a plant cell to their school. Listed below are a the definitions of the parts of a plant cell for your reference.

Cell wall – This outer barrier provides extra support for the cell and gives it a shape.

Plasma (Cell) Membrane – The cell membrane encloses the cell. It acts like a gatekeeper – allowing some materials to pass through it, but not others.

Nucleus – This structure, found inside the nucleus, is responsible for making ribosomes, which are then transported to the cytoplasm.

Cytoplasm – Cytoplasm is a gel-like fluid that takes up most of the space inside a cell. Cytoplasm is mostly water, with other substances dissolved in it.

Chloroplast(s) – These food-making structures of plant cells contain the green pigment, chlorophyll.

Mitochondrion – Mitochondria use oxygen to transform the energy in food to a form the cell can use to carry out its activities. These structures are sometimes called the "powerhouses" of the cell.

Vacuole(s) – These fluid-filled structures temporarily store different substances needed by the cell.

Chromosomes – Chromosomes are the structures located in the nucleus of a cell, made of DNA, that contains the genetic information needed to carry out cell functions and make new cells.

Ribosome(s) – Ribosomes are the structure in a cell where proteins are put together.

Working with Students with Special Needs

• **Work in a small group or with a partner.**
• **Use a definition list of the parts of the cell (like the one on this page).**

Name: _____

Compare A Plant Cell to Your School

Directions: In the space provided below, describe the function of each cell organelle and then state what person in your school serves a similar function and why.

Plant Organelle	Function Within the Plant Cell	Who/what at your school has a similar job?
Cell Wall		
Plasma (Cell)		
Membrane		
Nucleus		
Cytoplasm		
Chloroplast(s)		
Mitochondrion		
Vacuole(s)		
Chromosomes (DNA)		
Ribosome(s)		

Desert Dilemma

GRADE LEVELS
4-12

Materials Needed:	Desert Dilemma worksheet for each student or group
Advance Preparation:	Make photocopies of the student worksheets.
Objective:	Students will practice critical thinking skills as they analyze and discuss different priorities in a difficult situation.
Procedures:	1. Distribute to the class the Desert Dilemma worksheets, either individually or in small groups. 2. Review the situation and instructions as a class. 3. Allow students 10 minutes to rank the items listed. 4. Have a class discussion on how they ranked the items allowing students to justify or revise their own choices.
Extension:	Get the students to list the objects on the back of their paper and put a star next to each of the objects they plan to carry. Then explain in writing how they plan to use each of these items.

TIPS FOR Success: *This activity can be done as a class with one student giving directions, and the other students doing the drawing at their own desks.*

Desert
Dilemma
ACTIVITY SHEET

Name _____

Desert Dilemma

Situation:

While driving through the desert you take a wrong turn and drive 50 miles before your car runs out of gas. You are stranded wearing shorts, a T-shirt and tennis shoes. There is nothing around you but cactus and sand. The temperature is about 110° F in the shade. Your only hope for rescue is to make it back to the main road.

You rummage around in the car and find the 20 items listed below. You realize that you will not be able to carry all of them with you so you rank the items according to how important you think they will be in ensuring your survival and rescue. Place the number 1 by the most important item, 2 by the second most important, and so on, with 20 being the least important item.

Remember that you are in the desert and that the three essential things for survival are food, clothing, and shelter. Work individually, and later we will discuss your choices with the rest of the class.

_____ any part of the car   _____ sling shot

_____ sun glasses   _____ 50 ft. of nylon rope

_____ AM/FM radio   _____ boots

_____ blanket   _____ first aid kit

_____ lipstick   _____ pencil and paper

_____ a candy bar   _____ flashlight

_____ box of matches   _____ plastic garbage bag

_____ silk scarf   _____ hammer

_____ an apple   _____ a pack of gum

_____ a map of the state   _____ canteen of water

Following Directions

GRADE LEVELS K-2

Time:	15–30 minutes
Materials Needed:	Teacher Directed Instructions Following Directions Activity Sheet Crayons
Advance Preparation:	Photocopy one Following Directions Activity Sheet for each student.
Objective:	Students will follow oral directions and develop their listening skills.

Procedures:	1. Ask the following questions to discuss the importance of following directions:
	    A. When is it important to follow directions?
	    B. Why is it important to follow directions?
	    C. What could happen if you did not follow directions?
	2. Hand out a worksheet to each student and have them write their names in the specified place.
	3. Distribute crayons to each student.
	4. Read the instructions 1-5 found on the Teacher Directed Instructions. Make sure that students do not begin until the instructions have been read twice.
	5. Collect worksheets for teacher evaluation.
	
	Adapting for Students with Special Needs: Remain in close proximity to students with special needs so they can focus and hear better.

Extension:	Hand out blank pieces of paper and have students follow simple oral directions as the teacher gives them (e.g., put your name at the top, draw a circle in the center of the paper, make a line across the bottom of the paper, etc.).

Teacher Directed Instructions:

Following Directions: Distribute to each student a copy of the Following Directions Activity Sheet and crayons. Tell them to listen carefully while you read the instructions out loud.

Say: *"Listen carefully to what I say to do. I will repeat each direction only two times. Do exactly what I say."*

1. Find the square with the butterfly in the corner. Put your finger on the butterfly. Color in the triangle with your crayon. Put an X in the circle. Draw a circle inside of the square.
2. Find the square with the umbrella in the corner. Put your finger on the smallest square. Color the umbrella. Write the letter A in the biggest square. Draw a line through the middle square.
3. Find the square with the apple in it. Put your finger on the apple. Now look carefully at the triangle. Draw a line above the triangle. Draw a square inside the triangle. Outline the triangle with your crayon.
4. Find the square with the flower in the corner. Put your finger on the flower. Look carefully at the circles. Draw a triangle inside the top circle. Write the letter your name begins with in the biggest circle. Color the smallest circle.
5. Turn your paper over. Draw a big circle. Make this circle into a happy face.

Following Directions

ACTIVITY SHEET

Name:..

Guess
the Object

GRADE LEVELS
2-6

Time:	30+ minutes
Materials Needed:	Pencil Paper
Objective:	Students will practice their listening and oral direction skills.
Procedures:	1. Have the class draw an object as you give an oral description. The object should be simple like a toothbrush, pencil, football, key, flowers, umbrella, etc. 2. Do not identify the object by name until students have had a chance to guess what it is and share their pictures with class members. 3. Repeat the activity with students giving oral directions. 4. Discuss the importance of listening carefully and giving good directions during this activity. 5. Discuss other situations when it is important to listen carefully or communicate clearly.
Extension:	1. Divide the class into teams of two and get them to practice giving descriptions and listening. 2. Have students draw a simple picture using geometric shapes. If time allows, have them color their pictures.
Extension:	1. Organize the students into partners and instruct them to sit back-to-back. 2. Have one student give directions about how to draw his picture while the other follows the directions and completes a drawing on the back of his paper.

NOTE: The student giving directions cannot look at the drawing in progress and the student drawing cannot ask questions.

3. Have students change roles.
4. When they are finished, have students compare pictures and discuss which directions were easy to follow and which were confusing.
5. Get the students to complete the activity again with a different partner. Compare the second partner's drawing with the one done by the first partner to determine which time they gave better directions.

Find
Someone Who ...

GRADE LEVELS
8+

Time:	15 minutes
Materials Needed:	Find Someone Who... worksheet, one for each student (facing page) Pen or pencil for each student
Objective:	Students will talk with students in the class to find out information about them.
Procedures:	1. Hand out one worksheet to every student. 2. Inform students they will talk with the other students in the class to find out if they meet the descriptions found in the boxes. 3. If a student does meet a description, they will initial the box on their classmate's paper.

TIPS FOR Success: | *Decide beforehand if it is okay for students to initial more than one box. In smaller classes, this is recommended.*

Name: _____

FIND SOMEONE WHO...

Ask the other students in the classroom to see if they fit any of the following descriptions. Have the student initial the line.

___ Has more than five kids in his/her family.
___ Plays golf.
___ Likes to work on computers.
___ Lives with or near a grandparent.
___ Has traveled outside of the country.
___ Likes the color blue.
___ Was born in a different state.
___ Had peas for dinner in the last week.
___ Did not eat breakfast this morning.
___ Has a dog.
___ Has read all of the Harry Potter books.
___ Saw a movie in the theater the previous
      weekend.
___ Speaks another language besides English.
___ Has the same birthday month as you.
___ Plays a musical instrument.

___ Wants to be a doctor.
___ Is allergic to peanuts.
___ Wears contact lenses.
___ Works regularly as a volunteer.
___ Has milked a cow.
___ Has done yoga.
___ Has been camping.
___ Likes the same band you do.
___ Has red hair.
___ Has homework to do that night.
___ Plays soccer.
___ Had cereal this morning.
___ Lifts weights regularly.
___ Has an after school job.
___ Has green eyes.

Name: _____

FIND SOMEONE WHO...

Ask the other students in the classroom to see if they fit any of the following descriptions. Have the student initial the line.

___ Has more than five kids in his/her family.
___ Plays golf.
___ Likes to work on computers.
___ Lives with or near a grandparent.
___ Has traveled outside of the country.
___ Likes the color blue.
___ Was born in a different state.
___ Had peas for dinner in the last week.
___ Did not eat breakfast this morning.
___ Has a dog.
___ Has read all of the Harry Potter books.
___ Saw a movie in the theater the previous
      weekend.
___ Speaks another language besides English.
___ Has the same birthday month as you.
___ Plays a musical instrument.

___ Wants to be a doctor.
___ Is allergic to peanuts.
___ Wears contact lenses.
___ Works regularly as a volunteer.
___ Has milked a cow.
___ Has done yoga.
___ Has been camping.
___ Likes the same band you do.
___ Has red hair.
___ Has homework to do that night.
___ Plays soccer.
___ Had cereal this morning.
___ Lifts weights regularly.
___ Has an after school job.
___ Has green eyes.

My Favorite
Corner

Time:	15 minutes
Objective:	Students will determine their preferences.
Materials Needed:	None
Procedures:	1. The teacher will designate different sections of the room as corner A, corner B, corner C, and corner D. 2. The teacher will then ask students to determine their favorite option and go to the corresponding corner. 3. Allow students to mingle in the corner for a brief time to help them build friendships with other students.
Example:	The topic is favorite food. The teacher will assign corner A as pepperoni pizza, corner B as macaroni and cheese, corner C as spaghetti, and corner D as hot dogs. The students then will migrate to the corner where their food preference is. Give students a minute or two to discuss and build friendships with other students in their corner. Other examples: Favorite season: Corner A - Winter, corner B - Spring, corner C - Summer, corner D – Fall Favorite school subject: Corner A - Art, corner B - Science, corner C - History, corner D – Other Number of Family Members: Corner A – 3 or less, corner B – 4-5, corner C – 6-8, corner D – 9 or more Favorite ice cream: Corner A – chocolate, corner B – vanilla, corner C – cookie dough, corner D – other. Languages students can speak: Corner A – English only, corner B – English and Spanish, corner C – English and French, corner D – English and other. Pets owned by students: Corner A – no pets, corner B – dog, corner C – cat, corner D – other. Favorite music: Corner A – rock, corner B – pop, corner C – country, corner D – other.

TIPS FOR Success: *You may want to consider writing the corner options on the board so you don't have to repeat them.*

How Many are There?

Time:	15–30 minutes
Materials:	whiteboard markers
Objective:	Students will categorize and count their classmates in various ways.
Procedures:	1. Discuss ways that class members are alike and different (eye color, hair color, number of siblings, number of places lived, month they were born, number of letters in their name, favorite food, color, candy, book, etc.). 2. Make a grid on the board similar to the one below using one of the categories mentioned above. 3. Complete the grid as a class by having students raise their hands for where they fit in each category.

When Were You Born?

January	February	March	April	May	June
July	**August**	**September**	**October**	**November**	**December**

	4. Have students determine which column has the most and which has the least. 5. Summarize by explaining that all things can be categorized in different ways. 6. Get the students to decide another way to categorize the class and complete a second grid. 7. Discuss situations where the information from the grids may be useful.
Extension:	Assign students to independently make a grid categorizing the members of their family in some way.

TIPS FOR Success: *Developing an organized method for determining and recording grid information will help significantly with class management during this activity. For example, fill in the columns one by one by having students who should be counted for each column raise their hand as you come to it. Ask another student, who is not being counted, to count the hands raised and enter the number on the grid.*

Addition Facts

7 + 5	4 + 4	6 + 3	3 + 2	5 + 1	9 + 4	8 + 6	6 + 5	3 + 3	9 + 8
8 + 7	7 + 7	3 + 1	6 + 2	7 + 4	5 + 3	10 + 9	6 + 6	7 + 3	6 + 1
5 + 4	4 + 3	9 + 2	10 + 3	9 + 9	10 + 6	8 + 5	6 + 4	4 + 2	10 + 5
5 + 5	8 + 3	9 + 7	7 + 6	8 + 8	9 + 6	2 + 1	7 + 2	10 + 7	8 + 4
10 + 8	2 + 5	9 + 3	8 + 1	2 + 2	10 + 4	9 + 5	9 + 1	10 + 2	8 + 2

Subtraction Facts

7 - 5	4 - 4	6 - 3	3 - 2	5 - 1	9 - 4	8 - 6	6 - 5	3 - 3	9 - 8
8 - 7	7 - 7	3 - 1	6 - 2	7 - 4	5 - 3	10 - 9	6 - 6	7 - 3	6 - 1
5 - 4	4 - 3	9 - 2	10 - 3	9 - 9	10 - 6	8 - 5	6 - 4	4 - 2	10 - 5
5 - 5	8 - 3	9 - 7	7 - 6	8 - 8	9 - 6	2 - 1	7 - 2	10 - 7	8 - 4
10 - 8	2 - 5	9 - 3	8 - 1	2 - 2	10 - 4	9 - 5	9 - 1	10 - 2	8 - 2

Multiplication Facts

7	4	6	3	5	9	8	6	3	9
x 5	x 4	x 3	x 2	x 1	x 4	x 6	x 5	x 3	x 8

8	7	3	6	7	5	10	6	7	6
x 7	x 7	x 1	x 2	x 4	x 3	x 9	x 6	x 3	x 1

5	4	9	10	9	10	8	6	4	10
x 4	x 3	x 2	x 3	x 9	x 6	x 5	x 4	x 2	x 5

5	8	9	7	8	9	2	7	10	8
x 5	x 3	x 7	x 6	x 8	x 6	x 1	x 2	x 7	x 4

10	2	9	8	2	10	9	9	10	8
x 8	x 5	x 3	x 1	x 2	x 4	x 5	x 1	x 2	x 2

Division Facts

5)35	4)16	3)18	2)6	1)5	4)36	6)48	6)30	3)9	8)72
7)56	7)49	1)3	2)12	4)28	3)15	9)90	6)36	3)21	1)6
4)20	3)12	2)18	3)30	9)81	6)60	5)40	4)24	2)8	5)50
5)25	3)24	7)63	6)42	8)64	6)54	1)2	2)14	7)70	4)32
8)80	5)10	3)27	1)8	2)4	4)40	5)45	1)9	2)20	2)16

Survey
Your Friends

Time:	30+ minutes
Materials Needed:	pencil paper
Objective:	Students will survey the class on a topic of interest, create a bar graph to illustrate the results, and develop questions relating to the information collected.
Procedures:	1. Conduct a class survey on a topic of interest. (Favorite candy bar, color, professional football team, etc.) 2. Have students construct a bar graph illustrating the results of the survey (see example on the following page). 3. Have students write three questions that require using the bar graph to determine the correct answer (see examples below). 4. Exchange papers among classmates and get them to answer each other's questions. 5. Make sure that both the student who wrote the questions and the student who answered them are clearly identified on the paper, then hand in for teacher evaluation.
Example Questions and Bar Graph:	1. How many more students voted for Oatmeal than Oreo cookies? _____ 2. What is the total number of votes for Peanut Butter and Sugar cookies combined? _____ 3. Which kind of cookie received the most votes? _____

Favorite Cookie

Chocolate Chip
Penaut Butter
Oreo
Sugar
Oatmeal

1 2 3 4 5 6 7 8 9 10
11

Extension:	Get students to develop individual surveys to conduct outside of class. Assign them to survey 30 people, at lunch, during recess, etc. After the surveys are complete, assign students to construct bar graphs to be compiled in a book or displayed in the classroom for other students to see.
Notes for the Teacher:	Finding an organized way to conduct the class survey will help with class management during this activity. One method is to get students to write their answers on a piece of paper. Collect the papers and get one student to read the results while another tallies the information on the board. The students love to participate like this and it leaves the teacher free to monitor the class and deal with any disruptive behavior without interrupting the progress of the lesson.

It is also helpful in classes where students have not had much graph experience to model the bar graph on the board while they construct their own on paper. |

Sparkle

GRADE LEVELS 3-6

Time:	10–40 minutes
Materials Needed:	A list of level appropriate words to be used for spelling practice pencil and paper
Objetive:	Students will review the spelling of vocabulary or spelling list words through a group game.
Procedures:	1. This activity can be played as an entire class or in smaller groups. Start by having the students sit at their desks or stand next to them.
2. Give the class a word to spell. (You may choose to have them write the word on a piece of paper.)
3. Going row by row, get them to spell the word one letter at a time. Everyone must listen so they know what letter comes next when it is their turn.
4. After the last letter is said, the following person says "Sparkle" and the next person sits down, indicating they are out. If someone misses a letter along the way, they too are asked to sit down.
5. Those who are out will continue to write the words that are given on their paper and check them as the continues. The game can end at any point, but may continue until there is a final player.

What Kind of Energy?

GRADE LEVELS 4-10

Have you ever been told that you have too much energy? Did you know that energy can change from one form to another. Lets take a close look at the different types of energy.

Motion is known as kinetic energy. The wind blowing or any other time when an inanimate object does "work" (e.g., causes an action to occur) would be examples of kinetic energy. Potential energy is the energy of anything that could start falling. A rock sitting on the edge of a cliff is an example of potential energy. Potential energy and kinetic energy together are called mechanical energy. Any machine is an example of mechanical energy. Friction is the rubbing of one object against another, and that creates heat energy.

Listed below are some examples of energy. Next to the example write the form of energy that it uses.

1. Rubbing your hands together...
2. Walking across a carpet ....
3. Preparing to jump from a tree house ....
4. An airplane taking off ....
5. Riding a bike ....
6. A motorcycle ....

Now list an example for each form of energy.
1. Kinetic energy ....
2. Potential energy ....
3. Mechanical energy ....
4. Heat Energy ....

For the following activity, use these sources of energy: river current, tidal wave, tides, sunlight, sound, heat electricity, magnetism and catapult. Write the source of energy for each of the following:
1. Lifting heavy ships...
2. Transporting lumber...
3. Popping a firecracker...
4. Picking up paper clips..
5. Wailing sirens ....
6. Light from a lamp ....
7. Demolishing buildings ....
8. Using a microphone ....
9. Growing plants..
10. Echo ....

Vowel
Digraphs

GRADE LEVELS
2-4

Time:	5 minutes
Materials Needed:	pencil paper
Objective:	Students will become familiar with digraphs.
Procedures:	1. Explain to students that a digraph is a pair of characters used to create a distinct sound. 2. Add ai, ea, oa, to make each of the following a word: W__ __ t C __ __ ch C __ __ l D __ __ sy __ __ ch Dr __ __ m F __ __ st Fl __ __ t P __ __ nt N __ __ l S __ __ t S __ __ p St __ __ l T __ __ st

TIPS FOR **Success:** | *If you would like to make the activity go a little longer, have students write sentences using each of the words.*

What is Your
Name Worth?

GRADE LEVELS 8+

Time:	15 minutes
Materials Needed:	pencil paper
Objective:	Students will calculate the worth of their names and get to know other students names.

Procedures:	1. On the board write:
	
	    A = 1¢
	    B = 2¢
	    C = 3¢ ...
	    Y = 25¢
	    Z= 26¢
	
	2. Have students write down their name on a piece of paper and try to figure out what their name is worth.
	
	    Have students answer the following questions:
	    Whose name is worth the most?
	    Whose name is worth the least?
	    Whose names are less than 50¢?
	    Whose names are more than 50¢?
	    Can you think of a name that would be exactly 75¢?
	    What is the most expensive name you can think of?
	    What is the least expensive name?
	    What is the average value of the names in our class?
	    What is the median?

Letter
Scramble

GRADE LEVELS
3+

Time:	15-20 minutes
Materials Needed:	Paper and pencil for each pair of students White board and markers
Objective:	Students will cooperatively mix and match a set of letters to create words.
Procedures:	1. Move students into cooperative learning pairs (move desks together). 2. Explain that on the whiteboard is written a set of letters. They will have a certain amount of time (depending on how they are doing) to make as many words from the letters as possible. As the teacher you can decide if the students can use the letters more than once in the words. 3. Write the following letters on the whiteboard: A E I O U Y S H R T D M 4. End the exercise by making a list of the words on the board.

TIPS FOR Success:
1. *Walk around the classroom while students are working.*
2. *Set clear expectations for the students at the beginning of the activity.*
3. *Encourage each pair of students to contribute a word to the list on the whiteboard.*

Get as Close as you Can

GRADE LEVELS 8+

Time:	5-10 minutes
Materials Needed:	Paper Pencil
Objective:	Students will design their own mathematical equations to try to get a predetermined number.
Procedures:	1. The teacher will pick a random number (in the thousands or greater for upper grades, lower numbers for younger grades) and write it on the board. This is called the target number. 2. The teacher will then write down five other random numbers. 3. Explain that the students using the five random numbers will need to create a math equation that has an answer that comes close to the target number. 4. Example: Target number: 1,050 Random numbers: 5, 87, 24, 13, 9 Sample answer: (87 x 13) – (24 x 5) = 1,011

TIPS FOR Success: | *Be sure to walk around the classroom and encourage students, as this can be a difficult activity*

Just a
Minute

GRADE LEVELS
K-12

Time:	3-5 minutes
Materials Needed:	Timer
Objective:	Assess what students remember about the day's lesson.
Procedures:	1. Tell the class that you will select 3-5 students to talk to the class about what they have learned today. Explain that the rules for this game are that they must talk for one minute without pausing. 2. Students may volunteer or be selected by the substitute teacher. 3. Have the first student stand and start the timer when they begin speaking. Have students applaud when their time is up. 4. Adjust the number of students who speak to the amount of time you have left in class.

TIPS FOR Success: | *For younger students or students with special needs, you may want to adjust the time to 30 seconds.*

Glossary

ABUSE: The physical, sexual, or emotional mistreatment of individuals.

ACKNOWLEDGE AND RESTATE: A classroom management strategy that verbally acknowledges student protests or outbursts, then restates expected behavior. Acknowledging a student's comment validates them as a person and will often diffuse an emotionally charged situation. Phrases such as, *"I can tell that you"* and *"It is obvious that"* can be used to acknowledge what the student said. Transition words such as *"however,"* *"but,"* and *"nevertheless,"* bring the dialogue back to the expected behavior. *(e.g., "I can tell that you are not very interested in this topic, nevertheless the assignment is to write a 500 word essay about music and you are expected to have it completed by the end of the lesson.")* (See also **I Understand.**)

ANECDOTAL RECORDS: Records of the date, place, time, names of individuals involved, description of the situation, possible actions, action that was taken, and the outcome of the specific incidents. This is recommended in instances of illness, injury, severe student misbehavior, and emotionally volatile situations.

ANECDOTAL SUMMARY: See Anecdotal Records.

ASSISTIVE TECHNOLOGY: Devices that increase the ability of students to get along in society or that improve their quality of life (e.g., wheelchairs, computers, hearing aids, etc.).

AUTHORITARIAN: A teaching style which demands immediate and unquestioning student obedience to teacher directives. (See also **Coercive.**)

BEHAVIOR INTERVENTION PLAN (BIP): A plan written by the IEP team for an individual student that outlines specific procedures and practices for reinforcing positive behaviors and decreasing undesirable behaviors.

BLOOD BORNE PATHOGENS: Bacteria, viruses, or other disease-causing agents that can be carried and transmitted from one person to another through blood.

BLOOM'S TAXONOMY: The six levels of thinking organized by Dr. Benjamin Bloom. The levels are organized from the lowest level of thinking to the highest in the following order: knowledge, comprehension, application, analysis, synthesis, and evaluation. These levels of thinking are often used as a basis for developing and presenting thought-provoking questions to students.

BODILY FLUIDS: A term used for a number of fluids manufactured within the body, which usually refers to blood, urine, and saliva.

BRAINSTORMING: Teaching strategy to generate a lot of ideas in a short period of time. A prompt or topic is provided, then ideas are expressed freely and recorded within a given time limit. Evaluation of ideas is not a part of the brainstorming process. This strategy is often used as a springboard or starting point for other activities. (See also **DOVE Rules.**)

CAPTAIN: The role of group leader in a cooperative-learning situation. This person is responsible for keeping group members on-task and working towards the objective, sometimes also referred to as the director or manager.

CAPTIVATE AND REDIRECT: A two-step strategy for focusing the attention of a group of students. The first step involves capturing the students' attention by whispering, turning out the lights, clapping your hands, ringing a bell, etc. The second step is to immediately provide concise instructions that direct student attention to the desired activity. This strategy is often used at the beginning of the lesson or when making a transition from one activity to the next.

CLEANUP CAPTAIN: A role in the cooperative learning strategy where the student is responsible for supervising the cleanup of the group's area at the end of the activity or project.

COERCE: See **Coercive**.

COERCIVE: Interactions with students that attempt to achieve obedience to rules or instructions through the use of threats or force. These methods or practices intended to compel students to behave out of a fear of what will happen to them if they don't.

COMMON SENSE TRAP: A classroom management trap, which involves trying to motivate students to comply with expectations by restating facts that they already know (e.g., *"If you don't get started, you're never going to get finished."*). This trap is unsuccessful because students are not presented with any real incentive to change their behavior. (See also **Traps**.)

CONCEPT MAPPING: A teaching strategy for organizing information about a central topic or theme. Key words and brief phrases are written down, circled, and connected to the main topic and each other by lines. Concept mapping can be used to introduce a topic, take notes, or summarize what students have learned. "Webbing" is another name for this strategy.

CONFIDENTIALITY: Keeping personal information about students private (e.g., not discussing student grades, disabilities, and/or behaviors with others, except on a need-to-know basis).

CONSEQUENCES: A designated action or circumstance, either positive or negative, which is a pre-determined result for a certain student behavior (e.g., a student completes their assignment, the consequence is they receive a ticket for a drawing at the end of the day).

CONSEQUENTIAL BEHAVIOR: Behavior that has significant impact on the learning environment.

COOPERATIVE LEARNING: A teaching strategy in which students work together in a small group (3–5 students) to complete a project or assignment. Typically each group member has a specific role or assignment and every member must contribute in order for the group to successfully complete the assigned task. Common student roles include captain, materials manager, recorder, procedure director, and cleanup supervisor.

CRITICISM TRAP: A classroom management trap that involves criticizing students in an attempt to "shame" them into behaving appropriately. In reality the more students are criticized for a behavior the more likely the behavior is to continue because of the attention students are receiving. Criticism not only perpetuates inappropriate behaviors, but it also creates a negative class atmosphere. (See also **Traps**.)

DESPAIR AND PLEADING TRAP: A classroom management trap where a frustrated teacher resorts to pleading with students to get them to behave appropriately. This action communicates to students that the teacher doesn't know how to manage their behavior. This strategy is ineffective because rarely will students be compelled to behave appropriately in order to "help out" the teacher. (See also **Traps.**)

DISABILITY: A term that refers to conditions experienced by individuals that result in the individual having special needs. (See also **Disabled**.)

DISABLED: An individual with disabilities such as being cognitively impaired, hard of hearing, deafness, speech impaired, visually impaired, seriously emotionally disturbed, orthopedically impaired, or having other health impairments or learning disabilities such that they need special services or considerations. (See also **Disability**.)

DOVE RULES: Rules and guidelines for conducting a brainstorming session. D – Don't judge ideas, evaluation will come later. O – Original and offbeat ideas are encouraged. V – Volume of ideas, get as many possible in the time limit. E – Everyone participates. (See also **Brainstorming**.)

DUE CARE AND CAUTION: The expected level of care and caution that an ordinarily reasonable and careful person would exercise under the same or similar circumstances.

EARLY FINISHER: A learning activity for individual students to complete when they finish an assignment earlier than the rest of the class of when there is extra time before the next activity begins (e.g., crossword puzzles, silent reading, art projects, etc.).

ECHO THE CORRECT RESPONSE: (Questioning/Risk-Free Environment) A strategy used to generate a positive and risk-free class environment when a student responds incorrectly to a question. The incorrect response is acknowledged, then the question and the student's attention are directed to another student. Once a correct response has been given, the question is redirected to the student who gave the incorrect response. The student can now "echo" the correct response and feel positive about their ability to answer the question.

EMERGENCY SITUATIONS: An unexpected situation requiring prompt action to maintain or secure the safety and well being of students (e.g., fire, earthquake, bomb threat, flood, tornado, chemical spill, etc.).

EVACUATION MAP: A map designating the closest and alternative emergency exits, as well as the recommended route for reaching these exits from a given location. Such a map should be posted in every class.

EVACUATION PROCEDURES: Specified actions to be taken in the event that students must leave the school building due to fire or other emergency situations. Often such procedures include recognizing the evacuation signal, escorting students out of the building to a designated safe zone, and accounting for students once the evacuation has taken place.

EXPECTATIONS: Established levels or standards of student behavior. Traditionally referred to as class rules.

FACILITATOR: One who enables or assists another in accomplishing a goal or objective (e.g., a teacher facilitates student learning by providing instruction, materials, and assistance as needed).

FIELD TRIP: An educational activity in which students travel to a location other than the usual classroom or designated learning area. Often field trips involve the transportation of students to and from school grounds. Special legal considerations and supervision responsibilities are associated with student participation in field trip activities. (See also **Permission Slips and Supervision.**)

FREQUENCY: The rate at which an event or action occurs and/or reoccurs (e.g., a student leaving her seat to sharpen her pencil three times in twenty minutes).

GIFTED AND TALENTED STUDENTS: Students who demonstrate above average ability, a high level of task commitment, and advanced creativity. These students often function at a higher intellectual level than their peers of the same age. Special programs are often instituted to provide advanced learning opportunities for such students.

GRAPHIC ORGANIZERS: Graphs that help students organize information.

GROUP WORK STRATEGIES: Strategies that allow students to work in small groups while learning and teaching each other information.

HIGHER-LEVEL QUESTIONING: Asking questions that require more than recalling facts. Higher-level questions require students to synthesize, summarize, classify, compare, apply, generalize, and/or evaluate known information before they answer the question.

HOMEWORK ASSIGNMENTS: Worksheets, projects, or other assignments which students are supposed to complete at home after school hours. They includes both the completion of assignments started in class and independent "at home" projects.

I UNDERSTAND: A classroom management strategy used to acknowledge and stop student protests before redirecting the student's attention to appropriate on-task behavior, without becoming emotionally involved in the situation (e.g., Student: *"You are the worst teacher we've ever had."* Teacher: *"I understand that you feel that way. However as your teacher for today you are expected to follow my directions. Please open your science book to page 132 and begin silently reading the chapter."*) (See also **Acknowledge and Restate**.)

INDIVIDUAL EDUCATION PLAN (IEP): An Individual Education Plan is established for students with special learning needs. The plan is developed by a team, which includes the student, his parent(s), teachers, and professionals. It details the goals and objectives of educational services to be provided as well as listing the special and regular activities that the student will participate in.

IEP TEAM: A group of educational and related services personnel who develop, carry out, and evaluate the individual education plan, or IEP.

INCENTIVES: Student rewards that provide motivation for appropriate behavior (e.g., a fun activity after everyone finishes the assignment, a certificate recognizing student achievement, tickets for a drawing that are received for being on-task or working quietly, etc.).

INCLUSION: The process of involving students with disabilities as active participants in general education classroom activities.

INCONSEQUENTIAL BEHAVIOR: Student behavior, that may or may not be annoying, which does not significantly detract from the learning environment or prevent students from achieving learning objectives and goals.

INSTRUCTIVE LANGUAGE: Directions, expectations, or rules that instruct students regarding what they are supposed to do or how they are supposed to behave vs. detailing what they are "not" supposed to do (e.g., work silently vs. no talking, walk down the corridor vs. no running, quietly discuss this with your partner vs. don't talk too loud, etc.).

INTRINSIC MOTIVATION: Motivation based upon an internal and personal reward such as a sense of satisfaction or pride in a job well done.

JIGSAW LEARNING: When students first learn information in one group and then teach the information in another group of students.

KWL CHART: A learning strategy that begins by identifying what the learner knows about a topic and what the learner wants to know about the topic. A teaching and/or learning experience then takes place and the activity concludes with the learner identifying what they have learned about the topic.

LEAST RESTRICTIVE ENVIRONMENT: A term regarding the education rights of students with disabilities, referring to their right to be educated and treated in an environment and manner similar to their peers who are in regular education classrooms.

LESSON KICKSTARTER: Strategies that help a teacher to access students' prior knowledge about a subject.

LESSON PLANS: A detailed set of instructions that outline class activities for the day, including lessons to be taught, materials to be used, schedules to be met, and other pertinent information relating to student instruction and behavior management.

MAINSTREAM: The enrollment of a student with disabilities in a regular education class for the purpose of educating them in a "least restrictive learning environment" (See **Least Restrictive Environment**). Often involves individual adaptation of activities and assignments according to the specific needs of the student.

MATERIALS MANAGER: A student role during a cooperative learning activity responsible for obtaining and returning equipment, materials, and supplies necessary for the activity.

MEDICATION: Any substance, either over-the-counter or prescription, used to treat disease, injury, or pain.

MONITOR: To supervise or keep watch over student actions and behaviors.

MOTIVATORS: Consequences that inspire and encourage students to accomplish tasks or behave in an established manner. Motivators can either be tangible objects such as stickers, sweets, and certificates; special privileges such as being first in the queue, talk time, and fun activities; or recognition and acknowledgment of efforts through either verbal or nonverbal communication. (See also **Rewards**.)

MULTICULTURALISM: Any difference between students regarding race, religion, or culture.

NEGATIVE CONSEQUENCES: Undesirable actions or circumstances that are designated as a punishment when established standards for student behavior are not met (e.g., a student brings a weapon to school, the weapon is confiscated and the student is expelled).

NEGATIVE INTERACTIONS: Any teacher/student interaction, either verbal or nonverbal, that occurs when a teacher corrects a student's inappropriate behavior.

NEGLECT: A failure to provide a child under one's care with proper food, clothing, shelter, supervision, medical care, or emotional stability.

NONCOERCIVE: Practices and methods that do not utilize force, pressure, criticism, fear, or other negative motivators to achieve desired student behavior.

NONVERBAL INTERACTIONS: Communication that does not involve speaking (e.g., smile of encouragement, written praise, disapproving look, etc.).

NOTE CARDS: A set of index cards with one card designated for each school where you might be assigned to teach. On the card is listed the name of the school, school address, school telephone number, school start time, name of the head teacher and secretary, driving and parking directions/public transportation routes, and approximate travel time.

OFF-TASK: When a student is not appropriately engaged in an assigned learning activity (e.g., student is writing a note when they are supposed to be completing a crossword puzzle).

....

ON-TASK: When a student is actively and appropriately engaged in an assigned learning activity.

....

PACING: The speed at which students are expected to complete an assignment or the rate at which a teacher moves from one activity to the next, in order to complete a designated number of activities in a specified amount of time.

....

PERMISSION SLIPS: A document signed by the parent and/or legal guardian of a student authorizing permission for the student to participate in a specific activity (e.g., field trip). A signed permission slip must be received before a student can legally leave school property for a learning experience. (See also **Field Trip and Supervision**.)

PHYSICAL FORCE: The inappropriate use of one's body to compel a student to behave appropriately or in administering punishment for inappropriate behavior (e.g., hitting, shoving, lifting, spanking, slapping, kicking, etc.).

....

PHYSICAL AND VERBAL FORCE TRAP: A classroom management trap in which the teacher resorts to physical force or verbal threats and abuse to achieve desired student behavior. Not only are such actions inappropriate but in most situations they are also against the law. (See also **Traps**.)

....

POSITIVE INTERACTIONS: A favorable action or communication between teacher and student that recognizes student effort or appropriate behavior (e.g., a teacher makes a positive comment about how well a group of students is working together).

....

POSITIVE REINFORCEMENT: A positive interaction used to acknowledge and compliment appropriate student behavior for the purpose of encouraging the continuation of such behavior in the future (e.g, a teacher verbally praises the class for working diligently and quietly on a writing assignment).

....

PRAISE: A positive teacher-to-student interaction that acknowledges and compliments students regarding their behavior or accomplishments (e.g., Teacher, *"It looks like you've put a lot of time and effort into this project, keep up the good work."*).

....

PREVENTATIVE MEASURES: The actions or steps taken to avert the occurrence of inappropriate behavior (e.g., establishing expectations and engaging students in constructive learning experiences).

....

PROCEDURE DIRECTOR: A student role in cooperative learning responsible for reading instructions, explaining procedures, and making sure that the activity is completed correctly.

....

PROFESSIONAL DRESS: Clean, neat, and appropriate clothing attire for the teaching situation. As a general rule, jeans, t-shirts, sandals, and other casual clothing are not considered professional or appropriate for the class setting. You should always dress at least as professionally as your permanent teacher counterparts.

PROXIMITY: The physical distance between student and teacher, often used in classroom management, where close proximity or nearness to students encourages appropriate behavior and often stops inappropriate behaviors.

QUESTIONING STRATEGY: An instruction strategy that involves asking topic related questions and eliciting student responses. Successful and effective questioning involves using higher-level questions, directing questions to a specific student, and allowing appropriate pauses for student responses.

QUESTIONING TRAP: A classroom management trap in which the teacher wastes time and is drawn off-task by asking a student questions whose answers provide information unnecessary for stopping inappropriate behavior or getting the student on task. (See also **Traps.**)

RECORDER: A student role in cooperative learning responsible for recording information regarding the assignment including writing down activity results and other information provided by group members.

RE-EVALUATE THE SITUATION: To take an objective second look at class circumstances in an effort to determine if there are underlying reasons why students are unable to complete assignments or meet expectations.

REINFORCE: To encourage a specific student behavior by providing rewards or attention when the behavior is exhibited.

REINFORCE EXPECTED BEHAVIORS: To encourage students to continue to behave in an appropriate or expected manner by providing ongoing praise, rewards, or positive attention when they behave in accordance with expectations.

REMOVE, IDENTIFY, AND REDIRECT: A strategy for dealing with inappropriate student behavior which involves removing the student from the immediate learning environment, acknowledging disapproval of the inappropriate behavior, and providing specific instructions and expectations for future behavior.

RESTATE EXPECTATIONS: A technique requiring students to restate those expectations you put into place. A teacher should never repeat an expectation that students already know.

REVIEWING ACTIVITIES: Strategies used to recap important events and items students need to remember from the instructional day (e.g., listing homework assignments on the board, brainstorming things learned during the lesson, getting students to construct a concept map of what they learned from a lesson, asking students to name the things they need to remember and bring to class the following day, etc.).

REWARDS: Praise, tokens, or tangible items given to recognize student achievement, accomplishments, or attitudes. (See also **Motivations.**)

RISK-FREE CLASS ENVIRONMENT: A class environment where students feel comfortable sharing appropriate ideas and opinions without fear of being ridiculed or criticized for incorrect or original responses.

SAFE SCHOOLS POLICIES: Policies and/or practices adopted by a school district for the purpose of fostering a school environment that is safe, conducive to learning, and free from unnecessary disruptions.

SARCASM TRAP: A classroom management trap that involves making negative remarks aimed at belittling students. This usually results in a negative class atmosphere and bad feelings between students and the teacher. (See also **Traps.**)

SEATING CHART: A chart or diagram depicting the arrangement of desks in the class and listing the name of each student in reference to where they sit. A seating chart can be easily made using a file folder and small sticky notes. Get each student to write their name on a sticky note then arrange the notes on the folder to reflect where students sit.

SEXUAL HARASSMENT: Behavior that is unwanted or unwelcome, is sexual in nature or gender-based, is severe, pervasive and/or repeated, has an adverse impact on the workplace or academic environment, and often occurs in the context of a relationship where one person has more formal power than the other (e.g., supervisor/employee, or faculty/student).

SHORT ACTIVITY: Teacher-directed lessons or activities that require 20 minutes to an hour to complete. Often implemented when the lesson plans left by the permanent teacher are unable to be carried out or there is a significant amount of extra class time.

SPECIAL DUTIES: Extra teacher responsibilities or assignments in addition to usual class teaching activities (e.g., hall, lunch, or playground duty).

STARTER ACTIVITY: A simple project or assignment typically used at the beginning of the day or class period, which students can complete on their own without instructions or help from the teacher.

STATE THE FACTS: A direct and to-the-point classroom management technique that involves clearly and concisely stating student behavior expectations and consequences if the expectations are not met, then immediately instructing students to engage in an assigned task. This technique is appropriate for situations when students are testing the limits, willfully being off-task or making excuses for inappropriate behavior.

STOP AND REDIRECT: A classroom management strategy for dealing with inappropriate student behavior. The teacher instructs the student to stop the current behavior and then redirects the student by giving additional instructions (e.g., *"Jason, please stop wandering around the room. Sit down at your desk and spend the rest of the class period working on your homework assignment."*).

SUBSTITUTE TEACHER REPORT: A report written by a substitute teacher and left for the permanent teacher. It outlines the activities of the day, explains any deviation from the lesson plans, and notes student behavior (including inappropriate behavior the permanent teacher needs to be aware of and information about students who were particularly helpful).

SUBPACK: A box, bag, briefcase, or rucksack filled with teaching resource materials including personal and professional items, class supplies, student rewards and motivators, and activity materials, which a substitute teacher assembles and brings to teaching assignments.

SUPERVISION OF STUDENTS: To oversee all of the activities and actions of students in one's charge at all times and in all settings and circumstances (e.g., field trips, field trip transportation, break, assemblies, evacuations). (See also **Field Trip and Permission Slips.**)

THREAT TRAP: A classroom management trap that involves the teacher verbalizing drastic, highly undesirable, and often unrealistic consequences if students do not behave appropriately. The premise of making threats is that students will fear the consequences so much that they don't dare to behave inappropriately. However, most threats are issued out of frustration and the teacher often loses credibility when students do behave inappropriately because the teacher does not really want to, or cannot, enforce the threatening consequences they have established. (See also **Traps.**)

TRANSITIONING: Providing a clear course of action for students to change from one activity to the next. The process involves giving instructions regarding how to complete the current activity, what to do with the materials they are using, what new materials they will need, what to do with these new materials, and how much time they have to make the change. (e.g., *"You have one minute to finish your science crossword, put it in your desk, take out your silent reading book, and start reading. Please begin."*)

TRAPS: Any of seven classroom management scenarios in which the teacher becomes "trapped" due to poor or improper choices in dealing with student behaviors. Once in a trap the teacher loses some of their ability and authority to direct student actions. (See also **Criticism Trap, Common Sense Trap, Questioning Trap, Despair and Pleading Trap, Threat Trap, Physical and Verbal Force Trap.**)

VENN DIAGRAM: A graphic organizer that allows learners to compare and contrast two ideas.

VERBAL INTERACTIONS: Communication or other interactions involving speaking.

VERBAL FORCE: The inappropriate use of language, threats, tone or intensity of voice to compel a student to behave appropriately.

VERBAL PRAISE: The use of spoken word to recognize and/or acknowledge student effort, progress or accomplishments.

WAIT TIME: The elapsed time or pause between when a question is asked and a response is expected. A recommended wait time is 5-10 seconds. This allows students time to formulate an answer and verbalize a response.

WHISPER TECHNIQUE: A classroom management strategy in which the teacher uses a very quiet voice to communicate instructions and get the attention of the entire class, rather than speaking loudly or shouting to be heard over the class noise level.

Substitute Teacher Report

Substitute Teacher: _____   Date: _____

Phone Number: _____   Grade: _____

Substituted for: _____   School: _____

Email address: _____

Notes regarding lesson plans:

I also taught:

Notes regarding behavior:

Terrific helpers:

Students who were absent:

Messages for the permanent teacher:

Please let me know of any areas you feel I can improve to be a better substitute teacher for you.

Substitute Teacher Report

Substitute Teacher: _____   Date: _____

Phone Number: _____   Grade: _____

Substituted for: _____   School: _____

Email address: _____

Notes regarding lesson plans:

I also taught:

Notes regarding behavior:

Terrific helpers:

Students who were absent:

Messages for the permanent teacher:

Please let me know of any areas you feel I can improve to be a better substitute teacher for you.

Journal of Lessons Taught

Date	School	Permanent Teacher	Subject Taught

Journal of Lessons Taught

Date	School	Permanent Teacher	Subject Taught

Certificate

★ OF ★

Award

Presented to

_____

In Recognition of

_____

_____
Date

_____
Teacher

Privilege Card

The holder of this card
is entitled to

Authorized Signature

_____

Privilege Card

The holder of this card
is entitled to

Authorized Signature

_____